THE ROUGH GUIDE to
Blogging

ROUGH GUIDES

www.roughguides.com

Credits

The Rough Guide to Blogging

Editors: Sean Mahoney & Duncan Clark
Layout: Link Hall & Diana Jarvis
Picture research: David Ardito
Proofreading: Nikky Twyman
Production: Aimee Hampson & Katherine Owers

Rough Guides Reference

Series editor: Mark Ellingham
Editors: Peter Buckley, Duncan Clark,
Tracy Hopkins, Sean Mahoney,
Matthew Milton, Joe Staines, Ruth Tidball
Director: Andrew Lockett

Publishing Information

This first edition published October 2006 by
Rough Guides Ltd, 80 Strand, London WC2R 0RL
345 Hudson St, 4th Floor, New York 10014, USA
Email: mail@roughguides.com

Distributed by the Penguin Group:
Penguin Books Ltd, 80 Strand, London WC2R 0RL
Penguin Putnam, Inc., 375 Hudson Street, NY 10014, USA
Penguin Group (Australia), 250 Camberwell Road, Camberwell, Victoria 3124, Australia
Penguin Books Canada Ltd, 10 Alcorn Avenue, Toronto, Ontario, Canada M4V 1E4
Penguin Group (New Zealand), Cnr Rosedale and Airborne Roads, Albany, Auckland, New Zealand

Printed in Italy by LegoPrint S.p.A

Typeset in Minion and Myriad to an original design by Peter Buckley & Duncan Clark

A catalogue record for this book is available from the British Library

ISBN 13: 978-1-84353-682-6

3 5 7 9 8 6 4

THE ROUGH GUIDE to
Blogging

by
Jonathan Yang

Contents

THE BLOGOSPHERE

1. Blogs: The basics	3
2. The rise & rise of blogging	8
3. Finding blogs	17
4. Subscribing to blogs with RSS	23

HOW TO BLOG

5. Blog hosts	29
6. Server-side blogging	44
7. Audio, video & Podcasts	51
8. Design & add-ons	61
9. Writing tips	80
10. Increasing traffic	89
11. Money, money, money	99

contents

WHAT'S OUT THERE?

12. Journals & interests	111
13. Blogging & politics	124
14. Blogging & journalism	133
15. Educational blogging	138
16. Blogging & business	146

THE BLOGROLL

17. The blogroll	161

Index	193

The
blogosphere

Blogs:
The basics

What's a blog?

A blog, or weblog, is a special kind of website. The main page of each blog consist of **entries**, or **posts**, arranged in a reverse chronological order – that is, with the most recent post at the top. Typically, each entry is a short chunk of text, often with links to other websites, though photos are often included, and posts can also contain audio or video.

Typically, a blog will also include the ability for readers to leave **comments** – making the whole affair much more interactive than a traditional website – as well as a list of the author's favorite blogs, known as a **blogroll**.

The verb **to blog** simply refers to the act (or art) of posting entries to a blog, while the **blogosphere** is the term that has come to be used to describe the entire phenomenon of blogging – all the blogs, all the links between the blogs, and all the topics being written about in blogs.

What are blogs for?

For many people, a blog is essentially an online **diary** or **journal** – a place to post musings and record day-to-day happenings, perhaps to keep friends and family up to date. However, many bloggers focus on **online developments** rather than personal ones. Their blogs consist mainly of posts about – and links to – other websites, including other blogs.

It's these links between blogs that make the blogosphere such a dynamic, interrelated whole. One blog points to a news story or website, other blogs pick up the story and link to the original blog, and so on. In this way, a single interesting post can ripple throughout the blogosphere in a matter of hours. And, due to the fact that many blogs rank highly on search engines (see p.94), many casual Internet surfers with no particular interest in blogs may come across the story, too.

Naturally, a large proportion of blogs focus on a particular subject area – gaming, politics, flower arranging, whatever – while others are used primarily for displaying photos, music or videos. While many blogs are the work of individuals, others – including many of the most popular – are updated collaboratively.

Why "blog"?

Internet history is always hard to verify, but it's widely accepted that Jorn Barger coined the term "weblog" on December 17, 1997. Barger's website, www.robotwisdom.com, went live in 1997 and consisted of a collection of his eclectic links to news articles and websites. Barger, needing a term that matched his specific task, blended the

---

Merriam-Webster's Words of the Year 2004

Based on your online lookups, the #1 Word of the Year for 2004 was

Blog *noun* [short for *Weblog*] (1999) : a Web site that contains an online personal journal with reflections, comments, and often hyperlinks provided by the writer

words "website" and "logging" to describe his process of systematically linking to other sites from his own.

In 1999, Peter Merholz shortened the term to "blog." He wrote on his website, "I've decided to pronounce the word 'Weblog' as 'wee-blog.' Or 'blog' for short."

Before long, "blog" had entered the lexicon as both a verb and a noun. It was even lauded as the 2004 Word of the Year by Merriam-Webster (see www.m-w.com/info/04words.htm).

How many blogs are there?

It's very hard to say how many blogs exist. Most tracking software only notices syndicated blogs (see p.23) and fails to monitor blogs that use Chinese, Japanese, or Korean fonts, plus those which require password access. There's also the question of whether you include blogs which have been left to die after a single post.

As such, blog statistics range wildly. As of mid-2006, depending on who you believe, there are anywhere between eight and thirty million blogs lurking about the Web According to a recent study by Technorati (www.technorati.com), around 100,000 new blogs are created daily, making for a doubling of the blogosphere every five months.

These figures make blogs sound like they're a dominating online force, but in truth they hold the interest of but a fraction of Internet users. Despite so much recent attention in the mainstream media, most people you speak

Blog half-lives

Many blogs are started, briefly loved, and summarily abandoned. Jason Calacanis, founder of Weblogs Inc., estimates that less than 10% of blogs are updated regularly. However, over the next few years, Calacanis predicts that nearly half of everyone who currently uses email will have a blog, and that with blogs integrating themselves into the common routines of everyday Internet users, the percentage of blogs updated on a regular basis will rise.

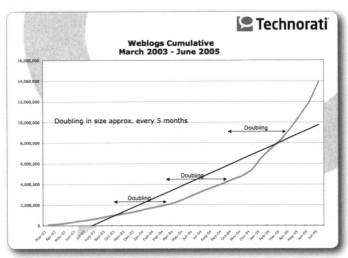

to aren't even sure what a blog is. Furthermore, recent studies have suggested that blog readership has plateaued, regardless of the continued rise in the number of blogs.

According to one recent survey, just over 20% of US Internet users read blogs, which would mean that the blogosphere's dedicated readership is roughly equal in number to the millions of people trading their wares on eBay.

Obviously, any new technology or activity takes time to be adopted by the masses. The Web, email, and digital photography were all the domain of tech-savvy experts relatively recently, and are now ubiquitous. Blogging looks to be heading in the same direction, but no one knows just how large the phenomenon will become.

Is it hard to set up a blog?

No, it's a breeze. Just choose a **blog host** (see p.29), sign up for an account at their website, pick a name for your blog, and you're ready to start posting. It really can be as easy as that. Even better, many blog hosts are free – though if you want a fully featured blog free from banner adverts, you might prefer to opt for a paid account. Alternatively, if you already have your own website, or you fancy setting one up, consider installing some **server-side** blogging software on your existing Web server (see p.44).

How are blogs updated?

If you sign up with a blog host, you create your posts using the simple tools built into the host's website. That means you can update your blog without any technical knowledge, and from any computer with an Internet connection. It's also possible to update a blog via a regular telephone, in the case of an audioblog (see p.52), or from a PDA or camera phone, in the case of a moblog (see p.43).

What's a permalink?

Most blog posts are followed by an inconspicuous **permalink**. This is simply a link to a "permanent" page where readers will always be able to access the post. This allows bloggers and other websites to link to a particular post, as opposed to the blog's ever-changing front page.

What's a Podcast?

A Podcast is, essentially, a radio-like show delivered as an audio file over the Internet (for more details, see p.53). Technically speaking, a Podcast is an audioblog delivered using RSS…

What's RSS?

RSS stands for "Really Simple Syndication." This is a clever technology used by many blogs – as well as news services and other websites – to allow readers to easily keep track of new and updated content. The site or blog creates what's known as a **feed**, which can be viewed either via a suitable Web browser or a standalone news reader. RSS can also deliver MP3s and other files, as in the case of Podcasting.

See p.23 to find out more about RSS, or p.97 for the lowdown on creating your own feed.

The rise & rise of blogging

In the space of just a decade, blogging has grown from a niche interest into something extraordinary – not just a popular hobby, but a new, bottom-up channel for distributing news and other information. Bloggers are challenging traditional media assumptions, influencing consumer trends, and putting the powerful on their heels. This chapter takes a quick look at this meteoric rise.

Goodbye homepage, hello blog

Before blogging became popular, personal **homepages** were the outlet of choice for individuals who wanted to create an online presence. Some homepages performed similar functions to today's blogs – they were updated regularly and displayed the author's thoughts or diatribes, links to favorite websites, movie and music recommendations, and so on.

Unlike blogs, however, homepages were cumbersome to update.

Revising a homepage required the site's owner to have at least a basic grasp of **HTML**, and to upload webpages and images to a server using **FTP**. This didn't require a huge level of technical skill, but it was a big enough barrier to put off most non-geeks.

This all changed when easy-to-use blogging tools hit the scene. Instead of having to sit through a session of updating your homepage bit by bit, a blog could be updated from any computer with access to the Internet without ever having to tinker with tedious code or mess around with an FTP program. Furthermore, the blog's chronological structure meant that anyone visiting the site could see at a glace what was new.

The first free blog publishing service was **Pitas**, which made posting to a website as simple as composing and sending email (almost). Pitas debuted in July 1999, and Blogger, Groksoup, Edit This Page, and Velocinews all followed not too far behind.

Blogging goes mainstream

With Web-based, easy-to-use blogging interfaces in place, the number of blogs quickly leapt into the hundreds of thousands. Such explosive growth helped fuel further technological advances, resulting in developments in the scope and design of blogs. Furthermore, the growing blogosphere necessitated new ways for readers to find good blogs, and in early 1999 Brigitte Eaton created the first blog portal, at www.eatonweb.com.

The previous generation of weblogs were primarily link-driven sites, but with more everyday people signing up every day, a new type

Links from the underground

Justin Hall is often described as the founding father of personal blogging. As student at Swarthmore College in 1994, he started posting commentaries about his Web discoveries. Over time, however, his site – Links From The Underground (www.links.net) – started to focus on his personal life, which he documented in the now-so-familiar format of dated daily entries. Hall didn't shy away from detailing romantic relationships, personal tragedy, and his struggles with medical issues, and he built up a big and loyal readership. In January of 2005, after an eleven-year run, Hall decided to stop updating his site, citing a lack of energy and loss of heart.

◀ *The first blog portal, EatonWeb, a couple of years after the first fifty blogs had been added.*

of blogger emerged – someone primarily interested in expressing himself in his own words. Dubbed **journal bloggers**, these people wanted to write about nothing more than the things going on in their lives – the trials and tribulations of attending medical school, holding down a boring job, raising children in a quiet suburb.

Others, however, used their blogs as personalized critical publications, where they could voice their opinions on politics, movies, books, music, sports, technology, and world events. These **pundit bloggers** grabbed dedicated readerships and served as hubs for communities of like-minded Internet users. A gadgets blog would provide not only the latest news and views, but also a gathering place for gadget geeks, who would interact by discussing posts in the comments boxes.

9/11 and the rise of the warblogger

By mid-2001, while blogging as an activity was gaining momentum, studies showed that blogs still represented an extremely small

Blogging: the final frontier

Politicians, movie stars, musicians, and other well-known figures have long been written about by bloggers, but since the turn of the millennium a growing number of celebrities and public figures have signed up for their own blogs, drip-feeding news and opinions to their fanbase. The regular updates and informal tone, combined with the ability to leave comments, made readers feel like they had a much more direct, interactive connection with these high-profile names than ever before.

One of the first "names" bloggers was *Star Trek* actor **Wil Wheaton**. He stumbled upon blogs as a way to express his views on showbiz and his post-*Star Trek* life, and, as it turned out, readers loved the former Ensign Wesley Crusher's lovable mix of honesty and humor. After some time, Wheaton started to achieve fame in blogging circles, winning the inaugural Bloggie Awards in 2001.

WIL WHEATON DOT NET
50,000 monkeys at 50,000 typewriters can't be wrong

slice of the Internet pie. In some sections of the media, blogs were being touted as the next breakthrough in publishing and communication, but the attention never quite penetrated the public consciousness. Leading blogs of the time were drawing upwards of ten thousand readers a week – impressive in its own terms, but tiny compared to the readerships of most newspapers. Blogs were still a novelty, a hobby, and few people were aware or appreciative of the growing phenomenon.

That all changed on September 11, 2001. The shock and devastation caused by the terrorist attacks on New York City created a demand for immediate and continuous coverage. Even with the

Where is Raed?

Salam Pax's blog *Where Is Raed?* chronicles his unique perspective before, during, and after the American invasion of Iraq. Salam started his blog as a way to keep in touch with his best friend, Raed. His site soon evolved to touch upon life in Saddam Hussein's regime, exposing and criticizing the conditions established by the repressive dictator. With the war underway, reports of Salam's writings from Baghdad came to the attention of newspapers in Britain and the US, and he became one of the most-linked-to bloggers on the Internet. The identity and veracity of Salam Pax was brought into question many times and was, for a time, a hotly debated topic on the blogosphere. Pax has recently worked with UK-based newspaper the *Guardian* as a journalist, including filming a series of award-wining reports that were transmitted by the BBC's *Newsnight* program.

traditional media working overtime, it wasn't enough for many people. Hundreds of thousands of readers flocked to personal weblogs to get the human perspective from the foot of the World Trade Center. Some blogs even posted minute-by-minute accounts of the tragedy as it happened, making for harrowing and intense reading.

The aftermath of the attacks pushed bloggers further into the spotlight. The question of if and how the US should retaliate was hotly debated by political bloggers, and, as the American military machine headed first into Afghanistan and then into Iraq, the term "**warblog**" was coined to describe the thousands of blogs focusing on the conflicts.

The structure of blogs served as an efficient means of exchange among pundits from both sides of the debate. By linking to arguments presented by other bloggers, or to articles from traditional media outlets, bloggers could react to an unending supply of news and views.

Naturally, this phenomenon wasn't limited to the US. As George W. Bush prepared the troops for actions, bloggers in the Middle East used their blogs to communicate with the rest of the world. Most notably, an Iraqi architect called **Salam Pax**, aka the **Baghdad Blogger,** captured worldwide attention with his from-the-ground thoughts and reports during the early stages of the Iraq war (see box).

The power of pundits

With ever more professional and amateur pundits staking their claims online (and the blogosphere proving a powerful tool for bringing sidelined stories to the foreground), politicians and main-stream media personalities suddenly had to deal with a new pack of independent watchdogs scrutinizing their every move. Blogs were being used as rallying points to both attack and support politicians and the traditional press, often with stunning results.

Trent Lott

In 2002, bloggers focused on radical comments made by (then) US Senate Majority Leader **Trent Lott**. In a speech celebrating the 100th birthday of Strom Thurman, Lott suggested that he approved of racial segregation, a view that was reinforced by documents and interviews dug up later by bloggers, most notably one Joshua Micah Marshall of www.talkingpointsmemo.com. By raising an incident that the traditional media had overlooked, bloggers helped to create a political crisis which eventually resulted in Senator Lott stepping down as majority leader.

Howell Raines and the *New York Times*

Just five weeks after the Jayson Blair plagiarism scandal broke in April of 2003, Howell Raines, Executive Editor of the *New York Times*, stepped down from his post, dragging Managing Editor Gerald Boyd along with him. Blogs proved to be very influential in orchestrating Raines' resignation, as widely read bloggers like Andrew Sullivan of The Daily Dish (www.time.blogs.com/daily_dish) and Mickey Kaus of KausFiles (www.kausfiles.com) consistently dogged the *Times* editor over errors in quotes, coverage, and content. Leaked memos and emails from *Times* employees made it onto popular blogs such as Romenesko, publicizing *Times* staffers' discontent with Raines and rallying further support for his departure.

Rathergate

On September 8, 2004, CBS journalist Dan Rather presented

andrewsullivan.com
"Freedom means freedom for everyone." – VP Dick Cheney

THE DAILY DISH
Email Article Print Version Black & White
IT'S OUR FIFTH ANNIVERSARY!
CLICK **HERE** TO MAKE A DONATION.

Saturday, May 10, 2003

THE BLAIR DISASTER: To their great credit, the New York Times has responded today at length to the frauds perpetrated in their newspaper by one Jayson Blair. Money quote:

A staff reporter for The New York Times committed frequent acts of journalistic fraud while covering significant news events in recent months, an investigation by Times journalists has found. The widespread fabrication and plagiarism represent a profound betrayal of trust and a low point in the 152-year history of the newspaper. The reporter, Jayson Blair, 27, misled readers and Times colleagues with dispatches that purported to be from Maryland, Texas and other states, when often he was far away, in New York. He fabricated comments. He concocted scenes. He stole material from other newspapers and wire services. He

documents on TV news program *60 Minutes* that conflicted with accepted accounts of President George W. Bush's military service record. The documents, acquired by CBS News producers from the late Lt. Colonel Jerry Killian's personal files, raised questions about Bush's National Guard attendance record. Immediately after the segment aired, conservative bloggers caught a whiff of something fishy, and declared the documents fake. Soon after, independent and rival news organizations picked up the story. Eventually, Bill Burkett, a former Texas Air National Guard officer and provider of the documents, admitted that he lied about how the papers came into his possession, but denied that they were altered or outright forgeries. With their informant discredited following a two-week period defending their position, CBS and Dan Rather were forced to apologize and retracted their story.

Howard Dean and Blog For America

In 2004 the United States was split down party lines, and that year's presidential election served as a focal point for pundit bloggers in both camps. While traditional online debates raged between conservatives and liberals, not lost in the hubbub was the story of Democratic hopeful Howard Dean. Dean employed a nationwide grassroots campaign strategy that relied heavily on his website and blog to help spread his message and raise funds. Using the Internet, he organized thousands of volunteers whose campaigning transformed him from the relatively unknown Governor of Vermont into a serious contender for his party's presidential nomination. Though Dean was eventually dismissed early in the nomination race, his use of the Internet, and the rallying power of bloggers, opened the eyes of many politicians. Today a serious Web presence is a requirement for any political campaign, and a blog written by the candidate is often used to give the politician some semblance of humanity.

Dean maintains a strong political presence on the Web, launching the Democracy for America site to promote socially progressive candidates at all levels of government and foster better communication within the Democratic Party. Naturally, the site has a high-profile blog…

Blog For America www.blogforamerica.com

Part of the culture

As the new millennium rolled on, it wasn't just pundits and politicians who were exploiting the blogosphere. Blogs were being added to many established websites as site managers realized the blogging's potential not just for keeping readers updated, but for making them feel "connected" with the site. Everyone from the UK's *Guardian*

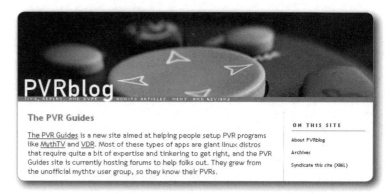

newspaper, via entrepreneurial magazine *Fast Company*, to the National Basketball Association, was getting in on the act.

Businesses were also starting to tap into the potential of blogging for improving relations with actual and potential customers, Microsoft's Robert Scoble being one example (see box). Similarly, businesses were finding their products and services under the spotlight of consumer blogs, a good example being PVRblog (www.pvrblog.com), which began tracking emerging recording technologies such as TiVo, Replay, and DVRs.

Even intranets – private websites maintained on office networks – started using blogs to keep their employees in the loop. All in all, blogs and bloggers had proven that they were here to stay. Once an obscure technological time-waster, blogs had become a genuine cultural phenomenon.

Finding blogs

Whether you're looking for a blog focusing on a particular subject area, or you'd prefer random diversions, there are various ways to locate quality content in the ever-growing blogosphere. For example, award sites are good for taking you straight to the very best bloggers, while blog directories can be useful for finding sites that don't score highly on traditional search engines.

Blog awards

Blog awards are given out in all sorts of categories by a variety of organizations. Some awards are standard fare – best writing, best photography, most humorous – while others are a bit more off-the-wall, offering up laudations for the most boring blog, the best use of wasted time at work, and the cheesiest smile in an author photo. The best blog-award sites include the following.

Bloggies www.bloggies.com
Panels of judges, multiple rounds of voting, and an annual presentation ceremony held at the SXSW conference in Austin, Texas, make Bloggies some of the most respected blogging prizes out there. Categories include

finding blogs

politics, food, technology, entertainment, best design, best writing, and the Weblog of the Year.

Weblog Awards www.weblogawards.org
The caretakers of these awards post the process of defending the polls from all manner of vote manipulation. Might electronic voting machines be so easy to crack?

The Webby Awards www.webbyawards.com
Internationally based and a decade old, these awards cover all manner of webpages, with subcategories for political, cultural, and business blogs.

The Diarist Awards www.diarist.net/awards
Awarded quarterly to the best representations of online journals. Categories include best comedic entry, best romantic entry, best use of multimedia, and best rant.

Best of the Blogs www.thebobs.de
Just registering to vote might net you an iPod shuffle.

Anti-Bloggies www.leiascofield.com/antibloggies
This site's disclaimer informs us that these awards are not meant to be taken seriously, and suggests we get over ourselves.

Blog review sites

There are a number of sites that specialize in reviewing blogs or pointing readers to particularly interesting bloggers. Two of the best are:

The Weblog Review

www.theweblogreview.com

The Weblog Review has evaluated more than 2000 blogs since its inception in 2001. The staff is comprised of volunteers, but they are, for the most part, knowledgeable and detailed in their assessments. Reviews used to be done on a first-come, first-served basis, and were generally turned around rather quickly. But, as of late, the staffers have been swamped by the number of submissions. To speed things up, they offers bloggers a pay-for-review system that guarantees a quick write-up – but not necessarily a positive one.

Blog of the Day www.shrednow.com/botd

Simple site with minimal descriptions of random interesting blogs.

Searching the blogosphere

The easiest way to find anything specific on the Internet is to type what you're looking for into a search engine. Finding blogs is no different – simply add "blog" your search terms. If you search Google for *politics blogs*, for example, you'll get hundreds of millions of results, with some of the best-known blogs featuring on the first page. And, of course, browsing each of the results will immediately connect you to even more.

Blog search engines & portals

As well as "generic" search engines such as Google, there are also various blog-specific search sites. These can sometimes prove more effective – not least because they have to comb through a smaller proportion of the Web, which means they can keep their results more up-to-date than those of the big guys.

There are also **blog portals**, or **directories**, that offer a browsable archive of blogs, arranged by category or popularity. Search and directory sites often overlap.

Tip: You can find the most-visited blogs via the website popularity index, Popdex: www.popdex.com

Tip: Search results can vary widely between two engines, so for maximum exposure to new blogs try a few different search engines.

Technorati www.technorati.com
The gold standard of blog search engines, Technorati boasts minute-by-minute tracking of over thirty million weblogs. The site displays which blogs are the most popular, what ideas are the most talked about on the blogosphere, and even offers a watchlist feature that personalizes your searches based on your dictated likes and dislikes.

Feedster www.feedster.com
One of the first RSS search engines on the Web, Feedster has maintained its popularity by providing searches of blogs, news portals, job postings, press releases, and items for sale. Feedster also offers a Podcast search.

Google Blog Search blogsearch.google.com
While search engines dedicated to blogs certainly existed before their entrée into the field, Google's 2005 launch of a blog search lent powerful heft to the genre. Even critics of blogging rejoiced, as blog results no longer featured in Google's standard search results. With a familiar Google interface, Blog Search lets you narrow down searches by subject, content, author, and date.

Eatonweb Portal www.portal.eatonweb.com

The first blog directory, Brigitte Eaton's Eatonweb Portal was started in 1999 just as blogs were taking off. She accepted link submissions based on one criterion only: the site must consist of dated entries. Her standard became widely accepted during a time when there was still a lot of debate about what defines a blog. Eatonweb is still the definitive blog portal, and you should add it to your blogroll if for no other reason than to share in a part of blogging history.

Blogpulse www.blogpulse.com

An established blog search engine browsing over twenty-five million blogs, Blogpulse includes a trend search tool, a featured trends section, and a popular conversation tracker.

Blog Catalog www.blogcatalog.com

A blog directory offering regional searches of topical sites with over forty categories to choose from, including pets, politics, philosophy, and Podcasting.

Blog Search Engine www.blogsearchengine.com

A blog-specific search engine featuring short site summaries contributed by a network of independent reviewers.

Daypop www.daypop.com

Tracks sites that update on a daily basis: newspapers, online magazines, and weblogs.

Ice Rocket www.icerocket.com

Lets you perform a general blog search, browse a topical directory, and tightly focus your output with advanced search functionality. The site also offers a Blog Trends Tool revealing in a simple line graph exactly how popular your query is.

Blog rings

A **blog ring** is a linked community of bloggers who have something in common – usually the subject they focus on. Each ring has a site that describes and links to each of its members' blogs. If you want to find a blog ring based on a particular subject – be it fly-fishing or the care of mullets – a quick search via Technorati's Blog Finder should do the trick.

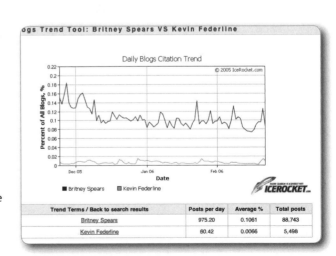

More tips

▶ **Use blogs to find blogs** One of the best ways to find good blogs is to follow links from other blogs. Bloggers regularly point to each other's sites within their **posts**, and most blogs also feature a **blogroll** – a list of preferred links in the sidebar of the front page.

▶ **Keep an eye on comments** Bloggers often include links to their own sites when leaving comments on the blogs of others. If someone strikes you as particularly interesting, insightful, or humorous in his or her responses, follow the link – you may discover a little-known gem.

▶ **Try something random** Most blog hosts and search engines offer a list of **recently updated** blogs on their homepage. It can be great fun to use these to dive into random parts of the blogosphere. Similarly, every blogspot blog (ie those hosted by Blogger) has a Next Blog button at the top of the page.

NEXT BLOG»

▶ **Explore the archives** While surfing quickly from blog to blog can be great fun, don't forget to delve into the archives of those you like best. Skimming through entries composed a year or six months ago will help you better understand both the style and content of the blog, and give you a better sense of the writer or writers in question.

The world's talking – are you listening?

Global Voices Online is an award-winning blog delivering news, information, insight, culture, and commentary from every wired country in the world. Their team of regional blog editors find, track, and aggregate "participatory media" – blogs, Podcasts, photoblogs, videoblogs – and display five to ten of the most interesting posts daily.

Global Voices Online
www.globalvoicesonline.com

Subscribing to blogs with RSS

4

RSS – or Really Simple Syndication – allows users to view "feeds" or "newsfeeds" from blogs, news services, and other websites. Each feed consists of headlines and summaries of new or updated articles. If you see something that you think you'd like to read, you can click on the headline to view the full story.

One advantage of RSS is that it saves you regularly visiting your favorite sites to check for new content – if something's been added or changed, you'll always know about it. But the real beauty of the system is that you can use a tool called an **aggregator** to combine the feeds from all your favorite sites. It's almost like having your own personalized magazine or newspaper.

When you "subscribe" to a site, you're essentially telling your aggregator that it should make itself aware of any changes to that particular RSS feed. As you sit back, your personalized aggregator will scan your favorite blogs and news sites for fresh content. All of this information is then presented on one screen, for easy consumption.

RSS tools

There are two main ways to view feeds. One is to use a piece of software on your computer. This might be a standalone aggregator program such as AmphetaDesk, or a Web browser with RSS functionality built in (see box).

The second option is to sign up with a Web-based aggregator such as Bloglines or Google Reader. You create an account, log in, choose which feeds you'd like to keep track of, and the website will create a customized page for you, displaying the relevant headlines.

Web-based readers aren't as fast and flexible as desktop-based systems, but they do allow you to access your feeds page from any computer connected to the Internet.

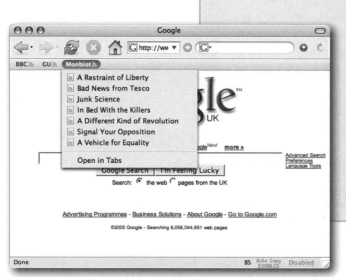

Web browsers with RSS

Browser plug-ins or standalone RSS aggregators have long been available to download from the Net. However, as blogs and RSS continue to expand in popularity, the makers of Web browsers have started to built-in RSS support. Safari RSS, for Macs, includes excellent aggregator functions, and the forthcoming Internet Explorer 7, for PCs, promises similar tools. Firefox, meanwhile, offers "RSS bookmarks," allowing you to quickly see headlines from favorite sites via the Bookmarks Bar (see picture).

AmphetaDesk www.disobey.com/amphetadesk

AmphetaDesk is a cross-platform, open-source aggregator that sits quietly on your desktop and downloads your feeds for display in your Web browser.

Bloglines www.bloglines.com

Bloglines is a Web-based RSS reader, meaning there's no software to deal with. Using Bloglines is extremely simple and is a great introduction to the world of aggregators.

Google Reader www.google.com/reader

Google Reader is still in its Beta (development) stage but is already a comprehensive Web-based RSS news reader. It has a clean, intuitive interface and offers excellent organizational tools.

How to blog

Blog hosts

5

Starting a basic blog is no more difficult than registering for an email address. You can have everything up and running within a few minutes. All you have to do is sign up with a blog host, pick a name, and you're ready to start posting. That said, if you're technically minded and want complete control over your blog and lots of extra features, there are various options to explore.

The best way to start blogging is to begin simply – and that means signing up with a **blog host**. The host will provide a Web address for your blog, various ready-made page templates, and easy-to-use online tools for adding or updating posts. You won't have to worry about anything vaguely technical such as registering and managing a domain name, learning HTML, or installing special software.

The alternative, more hands-on approach involves maintaining blog software installed on a Web server that you access directly. Known as **server-side** or **self-hosted** blogging, this option requires more technical know-how and takes longer to set up, but it offers far more features and greater flexibility. See p.44 for more information.

Naming your blog

Whatever type of blog you set up, picking a good name for your blog is absolutely key. The ideal name is memorable, stands out from the crowd, and means something – the sort of thing you wouldn't mind seeing splashed over billboards everywhere. A surprising number of people are inclined to name their blogs "My Life" or "A Day In The Life of Brian" – and a few of these are even successful – but a more original and engaging moniker will help attract an audience as well as buttress your online persona. Which blog would you rather read: "A Blog about Books" or "Bookslut"?

It may help to think of your blog's name along the lines of a superhero identity. Superman and Batman may have taken aliases to protect their civilian identities, but their names also provide a shift in mentality – Clark Kent doesn't save the world, Superman does.

Taglines

A tagline is similar to the advertising slogans used in movie promotions. The idea is to create a memorable phrase that sums up the tone and premise of a film. While taglines for blogs are hardly as permanent, a sharp, witty tagline will stick with readers, and a great tagline might be enough to encourage a casual Web surfer to stop and browse through a few posts. Compare these famous movie taglines with the ones that have been nominated for Fairvue's Bloggies Awards over the years:

Alien In space no one can hear you scream
Jaws 2 Just when you thought it was safe to go back in the water…
The X-Files The Truth is Out There

AllAboutGeorge One man's life: it's enough to make you URL
C:\PIRILLO.EXE Getting screwed while everybody else is getting laid
Metafilter More addictive than crack
Mighty Girl Famous among dozens
Tenth-Muse.com Fabulous since 1973, blogging since 2003, drinking since noon

Taglines can be located in the header portion of a blog page, or placed discreetly at the top of the sidebar. Another option is to put it within the page title – i.e. between the page's **\<title\>** tags. This makes it appear at the top of the Web browser's window rather than within the page itself. For more on headers and sidebars, see p.62.

GEEKSMAKEMEHOT.COM
I MAKE OUT WITH GEEKS

BIG NEWS

Sunday, February 19, 2006 at 8:49 pm Posted by: Jennifer
Category: Personal

My lack of posts have good reasons behind it. Tons of new stuff going on in my personal life. I'm seriously so happy I could burst!! Someone pinch me and make sure this is real.

Things normally do not go my way. My life follows Murphy's Law: *If anything can go wrong, it will.*

Well, I told you all that I found the perfect apartment. My new landlord comes by my work Tuesday afternoon. I sign my six month lease and pay my $200 deposit. We discuss me moving in Friday.

Two, maybe three hours later I get a phone call from the district office of my company. The posistion I've been working towards for three years is open again. I WANT this job, I am made for this job, this job has to be mine. I applied for this job a year and a half ago. Needless to say I didn't get it. I BLEW the interview. Interviewing is one of my stronger traits. I haven't a clue what happened that day. This will not happen again.
So I sit there in shock while listening to the "You apply online" ect. I'm so excited, but keep thinking back... I just signed a 6 month lease!!! (the job is in Memphis, TN). There is no possible way I'm not going for this job. IT WILL BE MINE!

So I get in touch with my landlord and tell her the situation. Ok, I think she must be the nicest person I've ever met. She tells me she

VOTE

Vote for "I make out with geeks" for Best Tagline of a Blog for 2006.

QUICKIES

Quote of the day ♥ 1

Today I was talking with Owen on Skype. We were making sure neither of us were talking too quiet or too loud. From this came my quote of the day...

> I get really loud when I get excited!

We sit there silent for about 15 seconds then both crack up.

I really need to think before speaking.

CSS for Kittens ♥ 0

CSS for Kittens by Bryan Veloso. The greatest CSS book ever!

HOME
ABOUT
FLICKR
LINKS
SITE
THEMES
ARCHIVES
GUESTBOOK
CONTACTS

Blog host basics

Blog hosting providers, aka blog hosts, offer the path of least resistance for publishing your content on the Web. They make the process of blogging streamlined and efficient right from the start – you can literally go from not having a blog to publishing your first entry in about five minutes. Blog hosts automate the processes of creating, editing, and archiving posts; they offer built-in commenting systems, spell-check, support for images, and many other useful features. After registering and setting up your blog, you can return and update it at any time, from any computer connected to the Internet.

The downside of using a hosted blog is that you may not have precise control over exactly how your blog functions – you're pretty well limited to whatever features they provide. Still, if you are new to blogging or not particularly computer savvy, this is the way to go.

Standard features

When blog hosts first hit the scene, they tended to offer only the most basic tools. But they've developed over time and today just about every host provides a decent set of features as part of the standard package. These include the following.

Tip: Almost all major blog hosts offer a trial package of their services with no long-term risks or commitments.

Blog addresses

When you sign up with a blog host, you'll be given a Web address within their "domain." For example, if you registered a blog called Rough Blog at LiveJournal, your address would be:

roughblog.livejournal.com

Or at Blogger, it would be:

roughblog.blogspot.com

However, some blog hosts, including Blogger, make it painless to use their service in combination with your own domain name, such as:

www.roughblog.com

For more on registering domain names, see p.45.

Free vs. paid

Many blog hosts will house your blog for free. The trade-off is that they'll usually display ads on your page – mucking up your carefully crafted design and distracting from your text – unless you upgrade to their paid account option. Paid accounts require a monthly fee (usually on the order of $3 to $10 a month) but your blog host will eliminate the ads and provide extra functionality. Try a blog host out for a few weeks and, if you like what you get, consider ponying up the dough for the enhanced version.

Source code

Blogs – like other webpages – are typically colorful combinations of text and images. Behind this fancy exterior, however, lies the "source code" of the page: a simple text document written in a programming language called HTML. The source code tells the Web browser how to display the text and images used on the page. You can see the source code of any webpage or blog by clicking the View Source command in the View menu of your Web browser. Thanks to user-friendly blogging tools, you don't have to understand HTML in order to maintain a blog, but it can be useful to know the basics. For more on HTML, see p.74.

▶ **Template-driven design** A blog template is a pre-designed page layout. Most blog hosts provide a selection from which you can choose, and it's usually not difficult to modify them by accessing their source code (see box). With the right coding knowledge, or by seeking out blog templates from a third party (see p.69), you can gain total control over what your blog looks like by changing **backgrounds**, images, fonts, colors, and more. Staid, generic blog designs are a thing of the past.

blog hosts

▶ **Draft posts** Posts marked as "drafts" are saved but not actually published on your blog. This is useful for unfinished entries you want to return to later, or for group blogs where an editor previews all the entries before they are posted.

▶ **Built-in commenting system** This allows readers to add comments in response to your postings. Most blog hosts also offer comment management tools, letting you edit and delete comments as you see fit. Keep in mind that some hosts require readers to register for an account before leaving comments on your blog.

▶ **Rich text editing** Also known as **WYSIWYG** (What You See Is What You Get), rich text editing means that you add formatting (bold, italic, etc.) and links to your posts with user-friendly buttons – just as if you were writing in a word processor. This way you don't need to know any HTML.

▶ **Spell-checking** Once the preserve of word processors, spell-checking tools are these days built into all kinds of software – including blog tools. This is useful, as nohting is more distracteng than numerous mispelled words.

▶ **Image hosting** Most blog hosts provide you with some online space to house digital photos. This makes it much more convenient to add pictures to your entries.

FTP

FTP (File Transfer Protocol) is a way of moving and storing files on the Internet. Most blog hosts will let you upload files to your blog using FTP, but to do this you'll need to grab a free FTP program (or "client"). See p.46 to find out more.

▶ **Flexible dating** Blog hosts allow you to adjust the time and date that a post is published, so entries that are written today can suddenly appear in last month's archives. And future-dated posts will remain at the top. While this can be extremely useful, it can also detract from the integrity of a blog's timeline.

▶ **Multiple archiving options** You can organize old entries by day, week, or month. Some blog hosts allow you to create individual archive pages for each entry or even organize your archives by category.

▶ **Syndication** Most hosts will automatically create an **RSS feed** for your blog, allowing anyone with a newsreader, or aggregator, to keep track of your latest posts (see p.23).

▶ **User profile page** With this feature, available from most of the big blog hosts, you'll get a separate page to display information about you – pictures, biography, contact info, your favorite movies, or whatever you like.

▶ **Post templates** If you tend to use the same fonts, image positioning, or code in your entries, you can save time by setting up a post template. This way, you won't have to plug in the same formatting details every time you post.

▶ **Email notification system** Many hosts allow readers to sign up for notification emails from their favorite blogs. Once registered, the reader will automatically receive an email each time you add a new post.

These features are offered by nearly every blog host, even if they vary widely in their presentation and controllability. One blog commenting system might let you choose to display comments alongside or underneath your post, while another might use pop-up boxes exclusively. It's wholly up to you to decide which you prefer. Remember, too, that feature sets for blog hosts are constantly changing, with extra features added all the time.

Which blog host?

Following is a quick look at what's offered by the major blog hosts. All of the services listed will help you get your blog up and running quickly, and provide enough tweakable features to keep you busy for some time.

Blogger

Launched in August 1999 by Pyra Labs, Blogger (www.blogger.com) was one of the first blog publishing tools and helped to popularize the phenomenon while positioning itself as the industry leader. Early success led to Google's acquisition of Pyra in 2003. With Google's resources behind it, many features that were formerly only available to paying users were offered for free.

Ad-free blogs

Blocky ads used to feature on all Blogger pages unless you paid a small annual fee to get rid of them. These were eventually replaced by a narrow bar at the top of the page featuring contextual ads, which was better but still intrusive. Fortunately, Google decided to do away with ads altogether on Blogger blog domains, replacing them with a helpful navigation bar including a search box, a BlogThis! link, and a next blog button that jumps you to a random blog. The bar is available in various colors, so be sure to pick the one that best matches your blog's overall aesthetic.

Blogger is often credited as one of the main reasons for blogging's explosion in popularity – and it's easy to see why. It epitomizes ease of use while offering a robust feature set for users of all levels. Comprehensive how-to's and help pages, moderator capabilities for group blogs, posting via Word documents – Blogger has it all. With new features being added all the time, Blogger is highly recommended for first-timers. By default, all Blogger blogs are hosted on blogspot.com.

▶ **BloggerBot** Google's purchase of **Picasa** in 2004 allowed Blogger to incorporate compatibility with the photo-sharing utility Hello. Featuring BloggerBot, Hello lets you quickly post photos to your blog – and also manage and search through the photos on your computer. This is especially useful for photoblogs (see p.178).

▶ **BlogThis!** This clever little tool takes the form of a BlogThis! button on your Web browser's links bar. When you discover an interesting website that you'd like to mention in a post, simply press the button. The link will appear in a mini-Blogger window, ready for you to add a few comments before you press Publish Post. The new post will go straight to your blog without you having to visit the Blogger website.

▶ **Word verification** By turning on this option, users can cut down on comment spam. A word verification step stops malicious software from being able to post rude or random comments to your blog automatically.

MyBlueDots

Tools like BlogThis! allow you to quickly post about online discoveries. MyBlueDots (www.blue.us) extends this concept while removing the "journaling" aspect of traditional blogs. When you find a site you like, simply press the "dot this" icon in your browser's links bar. If you want you can add a few comments, and the link – complete with thumbnail image – will be added to your online list of interesting places. However, your discoveries will only be available to members of your personal network (à la social sites like Friendster and MySpace).

Tip: If you highlight text on a webpage before hitting BlogThis!, the highlighted text will appear in the pop-up window, ready to be quoted in your post.

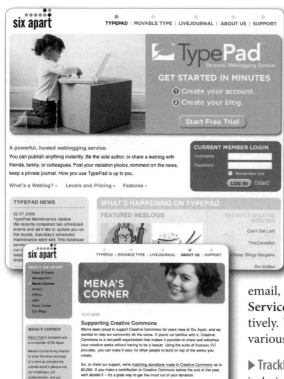

TypePad

TypePad (www.typepad.com) is the hosted alternative to Six Apart's server-side software Movable Type (see p.47) and it has attracted quite a following for its smooth interface, rich feature set, and well-designed templates. It comes with a full set of posting features, and will help you set up photo albums, automatically generating thumbnails and individual display pages.

You need to pay to use TypePad (after a free thirty-day trial period) and there are three levels of service: Basic, Plus, and Pro. Basic is $4.95 a month and gives you one weblog with unlimited photo albums, category and date archives, access to a library of pre-designed templates, and a laundry list of other features, such as posting by email, phone, or mobile device (see p.43). **Plus and Pro Services** are available at $8.95 and $14.95 a month, respectively. With these, you can host multiple blogs and access various extra tools.

▶ **TrackBack** Developed by Six Apart and popularized by its inclusion in Movable Type, TrackBack lets you display a list of everyone who has linked to one of your posts in their blog. Each TrackBack item includes a short summary of its target's content.

▶ **TypeLists** After inputting your favorite movies and music, TypePad will display a thumbnail and a link from Amazon.com in your sidebar.

▶ **QuickPost** Like Blogger's BlogThis! button, QuickPost puts an icon in your Web browser's links bar, allowing you to quickly post about a newly discovered website.

LiveJournal

Created by Brad Fitzpatrick in 1999 as a way of keeping his friends up-to-date, LiveJournal (www.livejournal.com) has since grown into a hugely popular blog host and online community. And in January 2005 it was purchased by blogware company Six Apart. LiveJournal is open source, meaning that, if you have the coding knowledge, you can tack extra on features as you see fit.

LiveJournal fosters a very strong sense of community, making it easy for you to join and organize groups with other members, and alerting you when "friends" post to their blogs. The site is well-organized, and lets users find people by region or subject. To-do lists let you to file tasks and projects, and, in a nod to the old lock-and-key-style diary, it offers built-in password protection so you can choose whether you'll display posts to everyone, to specific groups, or to no one but yourself.

Paid LiveJournal accounts cost $3 a month, $15 for six months, and $19.95 for a year. For this, you get an email account, a personalized domain name (eg. jonsblog.livejournal .com instead of www.livejournal.com/users/ jonsblog), advanced template customization, embedded poll tools with automatically tabulated votes, and multiple user profiles. You also get a site-tracking service that shows you how many visitors you have (and where they've come from), and **ScrapBook**, LiveJournal's photo hosting service.

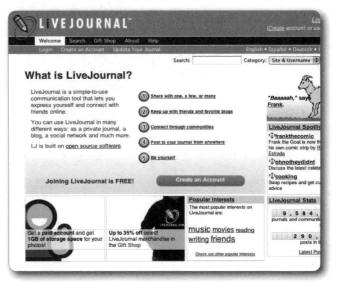

▶ **Text messaging** LiveJournal offers a unique texting service to its paying customers: once you've set it up via your User Info page, visitors

Frank the Goat

Frank the Goat, LiveJournal's official mascot, is no average caprine. His maintains his own blog (see frank.livejournal.com), helps out with "random programming," and even responds to the occasional tech-support call.

can simply click your texting link, and a box pops up where they can write a message that will be sent to your phone.

Xanga

Xanga (www.xanga.com) has powerful community and social-networking tools, and is one of the most popular blog host providers for teenagers and young adults. A free Xanga blog comes enabled with comments, a **guestbook**, pages for entertainment reviews, and an events page. To foster interaction among its users, Xanga makes it extremely easy to join blog rings and to subscribe to other users' blogs. Along with comments, users can award eProps to posts that they particularly like (see box).

Xanga Premium service starts at $4 per month and gives you more powerful versions of the basic tools as well as additional design and customization options. Premium members can also download a complete copy of their blog in case they want to store it somewhere other than Xanga's servers.

▶ **XTools Browser Button** Add this "bookmarklet" to your browser's links bar and you can use most of Xanga's editing tools without having to log in via the Xanga homepage.

And more…

If you tend to buck popular trends, perhaps you'd prefer a less mainstream hosted solution. Try one of the following.

Radio Userland

Radio Userland (radio.userland.com) is one of the most fully featured blog hosts. You have to pay to sign up, but it's well worth the outlay, as you get (among other services) directory organization, multiple author capabilities, email updating, an integrated news **aggregator**, and precise control over security. If somewhere between $99 and $1000 (depending on personal, corporate, or educational use) for the software and a one-year license period seems a bit steep, a free thirty-day trial will help you make up your mind.

Radio Userland differs from the other blog hosts mentioned so far because it's not Web-browser-based. The software, and all of your files and source code, are stored on your own computer, and updated to your blog when you choose to connect. This gives you the ability to compose entries offline – for example, when out and about with a laptop.

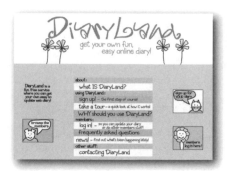

▲
*Diaryland is aimed at a slightly
younger crowd*

Diaryland

Diaryland (www.diaryland.com), which aims at a younger crowd, was one of the first blog hosts, and it offers most of the standard features as well as an email account that cleverly incorporates your blog's name in the address. Furthermore, even free accounts are ad-free. The same company is behind Pitas (www.pitas.com), a barebones host that is free and easy to use – ideal if you want a basic blog with no muss or fuss.

Myspace and Friendster

Myspace (www.myspace.com) and Friendster (www.friendster.com) are social networking sites that allow you to put up a personal profile and then link to your friends. Being friends with someone gives you access to otherwise undisclosed profiles, pictures, and additional circles of friends. Communities quickly grow as groups of friends become interconnected, and communication abounds. Both sites have become popular social hubs, with thousands of addicted users checking their profiles and messages many times a day.

Unsurprisingly, Myspace and Friendster – along with other social-networking sites such as **MSN Spaces** and **Yahoo! 360º** – incorporate blogging tools into the mix, offering feature sets similar to the other major blog hosts. In fact, Friendster blogs are powered by TypePad (see p.38).

Moblog hosts

Coined by Adam Greenfield in 2002, the term "**moblogging**" (mobile blogging) is used to describe posting content via an Internet-capable portable device – such as a mobile phone or PDA. Most commonly, it works like this:

▶ Snap a picture with a camera phone.

▶ Write a few descriptive sentences for the picture.

▶ Email the picture and the text to your blog.

▶ The blog is immediately updated.

It's really that easy. You don't have to sit in front of a computer to update information, and that translates into quicker responses from otherwise disconnected or distant individuals.

Buzznet www.buzznet.com

While primarily a photoblog host, Buzznet offers some of the best moblogging tools around. Users can create their own picture galleries and enable posting by multiple authors, and you can update your moblog via Web browser, email, or camera phone. Buzznet also offers archives and syndication.

EasyMoblog www.easymoblog.org

EasyMoblog is an open-source platform for publishing moblogs. It features customizable layouts, support for RSS syndication, and the automatic resizing of large images sent with posts, and it's very easy to use.

Text America www.textamerica.com

Another service offering blogs updatable via computer or mobile device, Text America does an excellent job of making moblogging simple and accessible.

easy moblog

EasyMoblog is an **open-source** platform for the publishing of personal weblogs and moblogs. With **EasyMoblog** it's easy to create customizable and easy-to-use weblogs with text, links and images.

...and is just as easy to keep it updated:
just send your blog an email!

| news | download | live demo | screenshots | documentation | contribute | team |

NEW EasyMoblog 0.5 is out!

With EasyMoblog 0.5 you will be able to set up your personal blog in **5 minutes!**

Updating your blog contents has never been easier: just send an email from your personal computer or your mobile phone, and **it will be automatically published on your blog!**

META-BLOG
the brand new weblog about EasyMoblog!

Server-side blogging

While blog hosts are amazingly simple to work with, they can also be a bit restrictive. If you want absolute control over your blog, then consider the alternative: "server-side" blogging software which can be downloaded from the Net and installed on a Web server of your choice.

The basics

To get started with server-side blogging, you first need access to a server – a computer that "serves" content onto the Internet. It's possible to set up your own computer as a server (see box on next page), but most people prefer to rent some space on a server run by a Web hosting company. You may even have some free server space provided by your ISP, though these may not be suitable for blogging software, depending on technical details such as whether your ISP allows you to run CGI scripts on the server.

Another consideration is the address for your blog. Ideally, you want your own **domain name** – eg. www.myblog.com – which means

Using your own computer as a server

Any computer connected to the Internet can in theory function as a server. However, in reality you need at least two things: first, an always-on broadband connection, and preferably a fast one; second, your IP address (see p.92) needs to be fixed, or "static". Many Internet-access accounts offers what's known as a dynamic IP address, meaning that your IP address changes over time. This makes it impossible (or at the very least difficult) to set it up as a server. Ask your ISP whether they offer static IP addresses; most charge a small fee for the service, though some offer them as standard.

Finally, you need some server software running on the computer. The most popular option is **Apache** – which is free to download for Windows and pre-installed on Mac OS X. See www.apache.org for more information.

registering it via a domain registrar for a small yearly fee. There are other options (such as using your own computer's numerical IP address instead of a normal Web address) but they're not really worth considering.

Domains and hosting

Unless you already have a Web address, the easiest solution is to sort out your Web address and server space (also known as "Web hosting") in one fell swoop. Almost any **domain registrar** will sell you the whole package, but before signing up make sure that the server space on offer meets the minimum requirements of your preferred server-side blogging software, as detailed later in this chapter.

Other factors to consider when shopping around are: the amount of space you're getting on the server; the monthly data-transfer allowance (see box); the number of email addresses included; and whether there's free technical support in case of problems. Finally, try to find out how easy it will be to install server-side blogging software. Some **Web hosts** – such as Fantastico and Dreamhost – provide click-through installation for Movable Type, WordPress and pMachine.

Popular domain registrars and Web hosts include the following:

Doteasy www.doteasy.com
DomainDirect www.domaindirect.com
Fantastico www.a2hosting.com/fantastico_hosting.php
Dreamhost www.dreamhost.com
123-reg.co.uk www.123-reg.co.uk (UK)

Once you've signed up, you'll need to grab a free FTP (File Transfer Protocol) program to upload your files and software to your server space. For more information about FTP, see the Beginner's Guide section of:

FTP Planet www.ftpplanet.com

Data-transfer allowances

Most Web hosting packages specify a monthly limit on your website's data transfer – or "bandwidth." Let's say you have an image on your blog that is 1MB in size. Each time that image is viewed by a reader (i.e. transferred from the server to another computer on the Internet), that counts for 1MB towards your monthly allowance; after 500 viewings, you will have clocked up 500MB (half a gigabyte) of data transfer. If you exceed your monthly allowance, you'll either be charged for each megabyte of data transfer over and above the limit, or your site be will be temporarily shut down.

Which server-side system?

There are many server-side blogging systems out there, though some are far better – and more popular – than others. The best options combine reliability and a good range of features.

Movable Type

Created by husband-and-wife team Ben and Mena Trott, Movable Type (www.sixapart.com/movabletype) includes a feature set second to none and is known for its sleek user environment. This is the engine behind blog host TypePad (see p.38) and the two share the

Movable Type requirements

▶ The ability to run custom CGI scripts

▶ Perl v5.004_04 or later

▶ An FTP program to upload files to your server

same basic features. However, Movable Type includes many extras, such as data import, multiple output templates, flexible archiving, search and replace... the list goes on. Because of the flexibility of Movable Type's customization options, you can put any variety of music, video, images or text on your blog, and make them do just about anything you want. There's also a large directory of **plug-ins** available, making it easy for less advanced users to add to their blog's functionality.

Movable Type has a free, unsupported version for unlimited blogs maintained by one author. Beyond that, you have to pay. Pricing depends on the number of authors, and whether the software is intended for personal, commercial, educational, or non-profit use.

WordPress

WordPress (www.wordpress.com) is relatively new to the blogosphere but has quickly gained a following. It has a clear interface and powerful features, including support for multiple blog authors,

WordPress requirements

▶ PHP version 4.2 or greater

▶ MySQL v3.23.23 or greater

▶ An FTP program to upload files to your server

Tip: Yahoo Small Business offer a Web hosting deal designed especially for bloggers, with WordPress pre-installed.

trackback, calendars, password protection, and searches – and just about anything else you could want is easily tacked on. Furthermore, WordPress is quicker to set up than Movable Type, Greymatter, and most other server-side blogware. Technical support is provided by the community of existing users. Best of all, WordPress is free.

Greymatter

The first server-side blog software and still free to the public, Greymatter (www.noahgrey.com/greysoft) was created by Noah Grey in response to traditional blog host constraints. After a few versions Grey stopped updating the software, but a group of open-source programmers continue its development.

Greymatter features a high degree of control over comments, support for multiple bloggers, customizable templates, a powerful search function, full editing capabilities, a polished interface, the ability to post from anywhere, and a diagnostic check that makes sure your files are working and organized correctly.

Expression Engine (pMachine)

As well as the standard server-side blogware tool, Expression Engine by pMachine (www.pmachine.com) includes unique features such as expiring entries, the ability to create printer-friendly versions of each page, multi-entry editing, and personalized HTML formatting buttons. One downside is that plug-ins, modules, and templates are harder to find than for established products like MovableType or open-source options such as WordPress.

Expression Engine is available for free to individuals, but there's also a paid version with enhanced capabilities, including tools to produce multiple blogs, various page templates, and **calendar functions**.

Greymatter requirements

▶ Perl version 5 or later

▶ An FTP program to upload files to your server

Expression Engine requirements

▶ PHP version 4.1 or greater

▶ MySQL v3.23.x or greater

▶ An FTP program to upload files to your server

Desktop publishing clients

If you like to compose your entries in a word processor before posting them, you may want to consider a desktop-publishing weblog tool. Posts are saved locally (on your computer) and then published to your blog at the click of a button. These programs tend to look and feel more like proper word processors than online blog editors, and they save you losing a post during an upload blip. Furthermore, they usually include tools for organizing multiple blogs and editing templates.

w.bloggar www.wbloggar.com
Free to use and compatible with most blog hosts (including Blogger and Movable Type), w.bloggar lets you use one interface to update multiple blog accounts, even if they're hosted by different blog providers.

BlogJet www.blogjet.com
Another multi-featured and easy-to-use desktop blog publisher, BlogJet has a thirty-day free trial but then costs $39.95 for a single lifetime license.

Audio, video & Podcasts

Gone are the days when typing was the only way to post to a blog. Audioblogs and Podcasts, which allow you to turn your readers into listeners, have quickly entered the mainstream, and videoblogging is touted by many as the next big thing.

Audioblogs

An audioblog is a blog that primarily features audio entries. They have a similar format to blogs, with entries catalogued by time and date. The only difference is the presentation, which is aural as opposed to visual.

The quickest and easiest way to audioblog is through a blog host that lets you post via the telephone. You can also create your own audio files and post them manually – this requires recording equipment and your own hosting solution, but gets around the time limits imposed by most audioblog services.

Podcasting versus audioblogging

The terms "Podcast" and "audioblog" are often used interchangeably, but there is a difference. An audioblog is simply a blog with, or composed of, audio files. Podcasts, on the other hand, are standalone audio files with an RSS feed. You can create a Podcast by adding an RSS feed to an audioblog, though the resulting Podcast will consist of just the feed and the audio files – not the written components of the blog.

Audioblog services

Audio Blogger www.audioblogger.com
Blogger offers an easy way to create an audioblog. First, set up a Blogger account, then go to the Audio Blogger site and set up an free audioblog account. Once you've registered, you will be given a phone number to call where you can start making posts –just call the phone number and start talking. When you're done, your recording uploads automatically. No muss, no fuss. You can make unlimited posts up to 5 minutes in length.

AudioBlog www.audioblog.com
Offering everything you'll need in one easy interface, AudioBlog is a full-feature audio, video, and **Podcasting** service. The cost for the service is $5 a month, or $50 a year.

AudBlog www.audblog.com
Audblog enables audio posting to your current blog via any telephone. You need a blog with one of the compatible hosts or system (Blogger, TypePad, Movable Type, and LiveJournal). A free trial is available, and the subsequent subscription rate is $3 a month for up to twelve four-minute posts.

Podcasting

A Podcast is, in essence, a radio show made available online as an audio file (usually an MP3). The term is a combination of "iPod" and "broadcasting", though this is something of a misnomer. Podcasting doesn't involve actual broadcasting as such, nor does it require an iPod – Podcasts can be played on almost any computer or MP3 player. Still, the term is catchy and has won out over more accurate descriptions such as blogcasting, audio magazines, audio-feed, and webcasting. Following in the footsteps of its big brother blog, "Podcast" captured Word of the Year honors in 2005.

The main advantage of Podcasts over traditional online radio – which is streamed over the Internet in real time – is that they can be transferred to a portable device such as an **MP3 player** or **iPod**. Furthermore, you're not tied to an inflexible broadcast schedule: once you've downloaded a Podcast, you can keep it for as long as you like, and listen to it at leisure.

Podcasts tend to consist mainly of spoken content – anything from informed debate on current affairs, recipes and poetry readings,

Feeds and files

The RSS feed for a Podcast does not contain the actual Podcast. Instead, the RSS feed contains a list of recent entries, or episodes, with links to the associated audio file. This linking feature is called an enclosure. Unlike email attachments that embed attached files in the actual email, a Podcast enclosure just points to the URL where the entire file is housed. This means that a Podcast's RSS feed doesn't consist of bulky **audio files**, but is instead made of very small text directions about where to find specific Podcasts. The settings on your Podcast software will determine when to actually download the entire Podcast.

to religious soapbox ramblings. They're mostly produced by individuals and hobbyists, and therefore sound less formal than professionally produced radio programs, though "real" broadcasters are increasingly getting on the bandwagon.

Listening to Podcasts

It's usually possible to download an individual "episode" of a Podcast directly from the website of whoever created it, but the idea is to subscribe to Podcasts you like using an aggregator or Podcatcher. This makes use of RSS technology (see p.23) and means you don't have to keep checking for new episodes of the Podcast in question. Your aggregator will check for new episodes at regular intervals and automatically download any that it finds. Podcast aggregators include the following.

iTunes www.itunes.com

The most popular aggregator by a huge margin, iTunes is also used for importing music from CD, buying and downloading music, and transferring tracks and Podcasts to an iPod.

iPodder www.ipodder.org
The original Podcast catching program created by Adam Curry. The site is also home to an extensive iPodder community that showcases Podcasts and provides technical knowhow.

Odeo www.odeo.com
Co-founded by Evan Williams, co-founder of Blogger, Odeo is not just an aggregator, but a tool for creating and publishing Podcasts.

jPodder www.jpodder.com
jPodder is a complete podcatcher program with robust features and a huge number of options available for customizing your listening experience.

Doppler www.dopplerradio.net
One of the first podcatchers for the **Windows** platform, Doppler remains popular and is widely used.

Nimiq www.nimiq.nl
A simple podcatcher that has all of the basic functions you'll need to download and organize your favorite shows.

Who started Podcasting?

Most of the credit for the rise of Podcasting has gone to former MTV VJ Adam Curry and blogging pioneer Dave Winer. Curry and Winer had tinkered with Podcasting since 2000 but found little public attention until July of 2004, when Curry wrote a simple program (latter refined by the open-source community) that automatically downloaded Podcasts to an iPod. Since that time, Curry has hosted and produced a popular daily Podcast on tech topics and remains the prominent public face of Podcasting.

Subscribing to a Podcast

Some of the above programs – such as iTunes – include directories of Podcasts for you to browse or search, and make subscribing as easy as pressing a button. But you could also visit a separate Podcast directory, such as those listed below. When you find a Podcast you want to subscribe to, you need to locate the address of its **RSS feed**, and then enter this into your Podcast aggregator. First, look for a button marked "subscribe" or "RSS." Right-click this link (or Control-click on a Mac) and select the "copy link" or "copy address" option from the pop-up menu. Next, open your Podcast aggregator, find the option for entering a new Podcast address, and press paste.

Podcast.net www.podcast.net
A well-organized directory with thousands of Podcasts in a wide variety of topics.

Podcast Alley www.podcastalley.com
A directory of 12,000 Podcasts in over fifteen categories, and a Top 10 Podcasts list as voted on by listeners. There is also Podcast software, a Podcast forum, and general Podcasting info available on the site.

Podcast 411 www.podcast411.com
A comprehensive site that features articles and references for Podcast listeners, creators, and the general public, plus links to more than a hundred Podcast directories.

Podcasting News www.podcastingnews.com
A blog providing Podcast news feeds from around the globe.

Weblogs.com audio.weblogs.com
A frequently updated list of the most recently updated Podcasts. Lacking descriptions or organization, this list boasts the "freshest Podcasts in the known universe". You can also subscribe to the list itself.

Creating a Podcast

If you have a microphone, a computer, and a bit of technological savvy, it's pretty easy to set up a Podcast. The learning curve is not steep, and all the software you need can be downloaded for free from the Internet. To get really good sound quality, you'll need decent recording equipment, but you don't need anything special to get started.

A full tutorial is beyond the scope of this book but, in brief, the process works like this…

> **Stage 1: Set up your hardware** You need to plug in a microphone to your computer. Most PCs and Macs have a socket for exactly this, but some don't, in which case you'll need either a USB microphone or an internal or external sound card.

> **Stage 2: Choose your audio editor**
This is the program you'll use to record and edit your Podcast. If you've got a recent Mac, you may find you already have GarageBand, a fully featured tool that's ideal for the task. If you have a PC or an older Mac, grab an editor from the Web, such as:

Audacity audacity.sourceforge.net
A free recording and mixing package for Mac and PC. Very popular and highly recommended.

MixCast Live www.mixcastlive.com
A Windows program created specifically to record and publish Podcasts,

> **Tip:** If you use Garage-Band, you'll find an excellent Podcasting tutorial on the Apple site: www.apple.com/support/garageband/Podcasts

MixCast Live is available for a small fee (currently $12) and provides a host of useful features.

Odeo www.odeo.com

Odeo has a comprehensive feature set for creating (and subscribing) to Podcasts. Odeo Studio allows you to quickly and easily record Podcasts through your computer's microphone, by phone, or with imported audio from any other viable source.

▶ **Stage 3: Record and mix** Once you've got your audio recorded, cut it down to size using the editing tools and finally export it as an MP3 file. If your audio editor doesn't offer this feature, save it as a wave file and convert it to MP3 using iTunes (www.itunes.com). If you're asked to specify a bitrate for the MP3, experiment with different settings. The higher the number, the better the sound quality, but the bigger the resulting file.

▶ **Stage 4: Publish your Podcast** Once you've created your first Podcast, you need to think about getting your audio file online and creating an RSS feed so that listeners can subscribe. It's possible to create an RSS feed manually (see www.audiofeeds.org/tutorial.php) and simply upload it to some Web space along with the relevant audio files. However, most people prefer to have the feed created automatically – often by using a blog host or software system in combination with **FeedBurner** (www.feedburner. com). This works with Blogger, among other systems, though bear in mind that audio files are quite big, so it's easy to exceed data-transfer limit. Alternatively, try one of these solutions…

Liberated Syndication www.libsyn.com

Liberated Syndication lets you upload audio (or video) files using a simple interface, and it automatically generates your RSS feed. It also gives you the ability to post text just on a standard blog. The service starts at $5 a month for 100MB of storage space.

Podomatic www.podomatic.com

Podomatic is a one-stop shop for creating and hosting Podcasts (and videocasts). It also offers podAmigo, an easy-to-use aggregator.

> **Tip:** If you make your own RSS feed, be sure to check it with a feed validator. This will check to make sure your feed is correctly formatted. See www.feedvalidator.org and validator.w3.org

Videoblogs (vlogs)

In the way that audioblogs focus on sound, videoblogs focus on video. With neither a widely accessible and uniform recording technology nor an effective way to distribute large video files, vlogging originally took a back seat to audioblogging. But, with the release of the video-capable iPod, and increased access to broadband Internet connections, vlogs have started to multiply.

The Videoblog Directory

The Videoblog Directory (www.vlogdir.com) is a well-organized site where you can find, watch, download, and subscribe to vlogs in over thirty categories. Vloggers can also submit their sites to the directory.

Vlogs are generally five to ten minutes in length and feature posts like cooking lessons, videos of local festivities, short films, family events, and hands-on product reviews. One of the best-known vlogs is Rocketboom (www.rocketboom.com), an irreverent daily news show.

Currently, there are no turn-key solutions for creating, publishing, and hosting vlogs. But if you want to get started for free, try:

Free Vlog www.freevlog.org

For more information on vlogging, try:

VideoBloggers videobloggers.org
VideoBlogging www.videoblogging.info
VidBlogs www.vidblogs.com
VloggerCon www.vloggercon.com

Design & add-ons

8

The design and layout of your blog can be as fantastic as your imagination and coding skills will allow. But simple is often best, and there are a few basic design conventions that should be enough to make your blog look like the work of an experienced Web publisher.

Basic elements of a blog

The header

The first thing a reader sees when they arrive at your weblog is the blog header, which is comparable to the "masthead" used to indicate the name of a printed newspaper. This introduction should set the tone for your blog and give readers a way to easily identify the site they're visiting. It might be a charming picture, a nifty graphic, or just text. Blog headers sometimes include links to non-blog

kottke.org home of fine hypertext products   ARCHIVES + XML   ABOUT   CONTACT sections of your site – such as an "about" page, additional writings, or a link to an RSS feed (see p.97).

Think of your blog as a budding brand, and try to show readers a logo, a motto, or something that will capture and maintain their attention. But don't overcrowd the header. Bloggers like to say, "If it's good enough to make into a header, it's good enough to put onto a T-shirt."

Sidebars

Most blog designs follow the classic two- or three-column layout, with the main column containing the blog entries and taking up most of the real estate. The narrow columns to the left and/or right of this are referred to as sidebars.

What you put in your sidebars is purely a matter of taste. The following list represents the most popular sidebar items found across 200 randomly selected blogs.

ARCHIVES + XML   ABOUT   CONTACT

Hi, I'm Jason Kottke. I like to play around with hypertext, design, photography, media, text, & programming, and this site is the result. Kottke.org is updated near-daily and recently became my full-time concern, supported almost entirely by financial support from you, the readers. Welcome.

About me and kottke.org | Contact me
How kottke.org became reader-supported

Remaindered links
I read books and watch movies
Photography (@ Flickr, kottke tag)
Silkscreen font

RSS: Main weblog | Remaindered links

sites I've enjoyed recently

Airbag	990000
Anil Dash	Acts of Volition
Assemble Me	Adam Greenfield
Blue Jake	Andre Torrez
Bluishorange	Andrea Harner
Boing Boing	Bitter Pill
Collision Detection	Black Belt Jones
Coudal	Cool hunting
Flickr blog	Cynical-C
Flickr friends	Daring Fireball
Google News	Design Observer
Gothamist	Dooce
Greg.org	Gomi no sensei
Gulfstream	Hello, typepad
Happy Go Larry	Jasonzada.com
Hchamp	Julia Set
John Battelle	Justin Blanton
Josh delicious	Justin Hall
Lightningfield.com	Largehearted boy
Magnetbox	Linkbunnies
Marginal Revolution	Mark Simonson
Matt's a.whole	Mike Davidson
Megnut	Morale-O-Meter

▶ A short bio

▶ A blogger's photo

▶ Frequently Asked Questions (FAQ) link

▶ "100 Random Facts About Me" Link

▶ A blogroll

▶ Links to other blogs by the same person

▶ Links to other Websites

▶ An archives link

▶ A search box

▶ "Today's mood" icon

▶ Daily quotes

▶ Trivia and other tidbits of information

▶ Current favorite movies, CDs, books

▶ An amazon.com "wish list"

▶ Donations button

▶ Advertisements

Posts

The blog entry, or post, is the main feature on your blog and you should afford it adequate respect. Don't squish your entries between information about yourself, your links, and your pictures from the weekend. Your blog entries are the reason people come to your blog and they should always be easy to read and navigate.

The look of your posts column will be determined by the entries themselves – form follows function. In a **photoblog** (see p.178), most of the space on the page will be given over to the main column, while a blog designed to update family and friends about your life might split the page equally between the posts column, a pictures column, and a calendar.

In general, however, the posts column should take up about 75% of the screen. So assuming your blog is 750 pixels across and designed as a three-column layout, you should make your two sidebars 150 pixels wide, and set the main column at 450 pixels. A main column less than 300 pixels wide will reduce you to a handful of words per line.

As discussed below, font size and style will also affect the dimensions of your blog.

The footer

Many bloggers add a footer at the base of their page. This is most commonly used to link to the tools used in the creation of the blog (the host or blogware, the comments system, the search box provider, etc.), plus a copyright notice and perhaps a **Web counter** icon

Tip: Putting "SPAM" in your email address can help cut down on junk email received. For example, if your address is shiwani@gmail.com, you might want to use shiwani@SPAMgmail.com for the purposes of your blog. Most human readers will understand your strategy and remove the "SPAM" portion of the address before pressing send, but spam software usually won't.

You're visiting kottke.org. All content by Jason Kottke (contact me) unless otherwise noted, with some restrictions on its use. Good luck will come to those who dig around in the archives. If you've reached this point by accident, I suggest panic.

kottke.org

Basic elements of a post

Blog posts vary widely in design, but most consist of the same basic elements: a post title, the date and time, the main text – including any links, credits, and pull quotes – blog author name, a permanent link, and an add a comment link. Let's take a look at these in turn.

Date

Post Title
Commentary
"Pull Quote" (Link)
Posted by Author @ Time, Add a Comment Permalink

▶ **Post Title** The title of your post is the headline for your entry. Keep it short, keep it informative, and set it off from the rest of your text by putting it on its own line. Most bloggers make the post title bold and/or use a type size that's slightly larger than the regular entry text. An interesting or humorous title can also draw attention to your entry and potentially convince browsers to stop in for a quick read.

February 25, 2006

Blogging 101
I found this great site about how to blog.
"When starting a blog, be sure to..." (Link)
Posted by Jon @ 5:35pm Comment #

▶ **Date and Time** The defining trait of a traditional blog is its reverse chronological format. Typically, the date is displayed above the entire entry while the **date and time stamp** sit below, on the same line as the blog author, permalink, and comment link.

▶ **Links and credits** Most blog entries link to other sites and blogs – that's what the blogosphere is all about. Bear in mind, however, that if you discover a great new site via another blogger, you should always credit your source. So, if you see something interesting linked to on Jon's blog and want to share it with your readers, give Jon credit for doing the leg work – including a link to the post in question.

FEBRUARY 04, 2006

MATTHEW YGLESIAS has joined **BloggingHeadsTV**. He's good, too!

I think that this is one of the coolest new things on the web, and if I were, say, Chris Matthews, I'd be worried.
                                          posted at 08:49 AM by **Glenn Reynolds** ●

TERRY HEATON ON NEW MEDIA: So what do you do when the deer have guns? You **go into the ammunition business.**
                                          posted at 08:47 AM by **Glenn Reynolds** ●

ARIANNA HUFFINGTON **targets Chris Matthews.** He seems to be taking fire from all directions these days.
                                          posted at 08:46 AM by **Glenn Reynolds** ●

▶ **Pull Quote** When you link to a story or an article you'll often want to include an excerpt from the source. In journalism lingo this excerpt is called a pull quote. Teasers meant to entice readers into clicking through to the linked sites, pull quotes should be set off from the rest of your entry (usually by being indented) to provide a visual contrast between what you've written and what you've excerpted from the cited article.

▶ **Blog Author Name** Otherwise referred to as a display name, your blog author name typically appears after each entry. This can be your full name, a first name, initials, a nickname, or a pseudonym. It's a good idea to link your blog author name to an email function, so when readers click on your blog author name a new email window will open with your chosen email address already in the To: field (see p.76 to find out how).

▶ **Permanent Link ("permalink")** A permalink allows a post to be associated with a specific Web address in your archives. This is important because it gives a fixed address that lets other bloggers link to that particular post. Permalinks are usually located at the end of an entry and can be incorporated into the time stamp or simply denoted by the # symbol. For more on archives, see p.73.

▶ **Comments Link** The **Add Comment** link allows visitors to post comments about specific entries on your blog. Many blog authors even use the comments section to conduct conversations with their readers. Comments can be hosted by the blog provider or by outside companies. For more on comments, see p.70.

More Employment Opportunities for J-Students
READ MORE: EDUCATION, J-SCHOO, JOBS, NYU

7 FEB 2006 ▼

Meanwhile, at NYU:

From: [redacted]
To: Journalism Undergrad Announcements
Sent: Tuesday, February 07, 2006 1:31 PM
Subject: quick way to make $30 NOW

Would anyone be interested in earning $10 by picking my child up from school on 22nd Street, taking him to tennis lessons on 28th St. and bringing him back to 10 WPL. It would be about a 3 hour job & I will pay for bus fare. You should be back on campus by 5:45.

Let me know asap if this works for you.

It'll be good practice for office cleaning you'll do in grad school.

Earlier: But Do Columbia J-Schoolers Do Windows?

(3 comments) 💬 ✉ 🔖

You're Safired!
Wes Felter calls for the ass fact-checking of William Safire over the latter's article in the NY Times about blog jargon and he's not wrong. Wes correctly notes the etymology of "weblog" and "blog" and hopefully the people responsible for things like the AP Style Guide, English dictionaries, and influential columns like On Language will, at some point, do the 20 minutes of research necessary to convince them and the unwashed journalist masses that "blog" is not and was never short for "web log".

Safire also gets tripped up on where the word "blogosphere" came from. While William Quick's usage in 2002 popularized the term, Brad Graham first used the term in 1999.

▤ Feb 19, 2006

and email link. However, some bloggers prefer to leave out all this information, while others add it to the end of a sidebar.

Fonts

Choosing the right typeface for your blog copy is very important – a font can connote a serious and formal tone, or a friendly and casual one. But, while thousands of fonts exist, only a handful are viable solutions for online use. The problem is, unless you employ some complex Web technologies, you're limited to fonts installed on the average Mac or PC. If you use a font that isn't installed on the reader's computer, the text will simply appear in a different font – either the default system font or something else specified in your HTML as a backup.

Another consideration is **readability**. A fancy font may be OK for headings, but you should never use anything too distracting for body text, which should be as easy to read as possible. Furthermore, some fonts that look OK on paper work less well on screen.

Images as text

For text that you want to present in a non-standard font – your blog header, for example – the best option is to save the text as an image (in JPEG or GIF format) using a program such as Photoshop. Much of the "text" you see on-line actual consists of images.

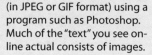

Common fonts for online use

There are two main types of fonts: serif and sans serif. A serif font is one that has "feet" – extensions at the ends of characters' strokes. A sans serif font, by contract, lacks these feet (*sans* is French for "without"). For online use, the most common serif fonts are Times New Roman and Georgia, while Arial and Verdana are the most popular sans serifs. Courier New is also widely used.

▶ **Times New Roman** Times New Roman looks serious and professional, and is widely used for essays and other formal print documents. It's also widely used on the Web, though it can be hard to read at sizes smaller than 12pt.

▶ **Georgia** Georgia was created when the need for a serif font with better on-screen readability than Times New Roman became obvious. It's elegant as well as functional.

▶ **Arial** Arial is almost universally available and is probably the most widely used sans serif font on the Web. Arial has good readability but at small sizes can become very narrow, with little space between characters.

▶ **Verdana** Verdana is probably the best sans serif font for on-screen readability, especially at small sizes. Widely available and created when the Internet was expanding exponentially, it looks modern and professional.

▶ **Courier New** Similar to the fonts used by mechanical typewriters, Courier New retains an old-fashioned appeal and is easily readable until you get to really small sizes. Courier New is useful for simulating computer code and for imparting a nostalgic feel to your blog.

> **Tip:** Many of us were taught to use two spaces after a period (full stop), but this is a remnant of the typewriter era. Modern digital typefaces use proportional fonts that take into account differences in the sizes of letters and symbols, and one space is sufficient after all punctuation. Even if you do write double spaces in your posts, they'll usually appear as a single space on your blog.

From a usability perspective, the winners are Verdana for sans serif fonts and Georgia if you choose to go the serif font route. Arial is a popular choice for headlines and titles because it looks best at larger sizes. Whichever font you choose, make sure that it won't distract your readers from your content.

Font sizes

All font sizes are not created equal. The heft of your type is denoted by a **pixel size**, and can range from 8 pixels to 48 pixels and beyond. The same pixel size will render each font differently, so your 8 pixel Georgia may be more legible than your 8 pixel Verdana – whatever the case, experiment with sizing to optimize readability.

Small type is not without its uses. Blogrolls, links, time stamps, author names, permalinks, and comment links can be written in tiny, slightly illegible, font because it isn't necessary to focus on these items for an extended amount of time.

Pixels and points

Font sizes can be specified either in pixels or points. Points are used in print publishing, where 72 points take up one inch of the printed page, but for online use it's generally better to use pixels, which are set relative to the reader's screen resolution. If this seems confusing, don't despair – point and pixel sizes are similar at standard screen resolutions, so it won't make all that much difference which you use.

Changing templates

Templates are the blueprint for your blog, and give your main page and all of its subsequent archive pages a uniform look. Templates are written in HTML, with Javascript, XTML, CSS, and other advanced programming languages providing additional bells and whistles.

Different templates can provide drastically different visual identities, so find one that reflects the personality and the tone of your blog. Templates are also referred to as skins, and changing a template is often called **skinning**. Your blog host will provide some stock skins for you, but there are many other sites that offer both free and paid alternatives. Changing your skin from time to time can keep your blog fresh and exciting, though too many changes might suggest some form of instability.

BlogSkins www.blogskins.com
A huge collection of blog templates contributed by a wide community of designers.

Template Hunter www.templatehunter.com
Offers free or paid templates, clear installation instructions, and a large directory of webmaster resources.

CreateBlog www.createblog.com
Houses free layouts, scripts, tutorials, and more, for all the major blog hosts.

Not (that) Ugly not-that-ugly.co.uk
An outcropping of a Diaryland-specific template resource, now offering templates for all blog providers.

Comment boxes from Blogger (top) and third-party provider Yaccs (below)

▼

Comments

Installing a comment system in the early days of blogging was strictly do-it-yourself, and most hosted blogs used third-party resources to manage their comments. These systems were generally created by hobbyists, and installing comments involved copying lines of code into the appropriate places in your blog template.

These days bloggers have it easy – most blog providers have a commenting system integrated into their basic package. The downside to using a blog provider's integrated commenting system is that sometimes they force potential commenters to create an account before they can leave their remarks – which is often enough to put people off.

Dealing with comment spam

Just as with email, spam in blog comments systems has become a major pain. Bloggers increasingly find themselves bombarded with comments that end with a link to an unrelated commercial site. This has been a particular problem for Blogger users in recent years.

Haloscan

One of the simplest (and still independent) commenting solutions, Haloscan is a free service that allows you to install, design, and manage a comment box. Haloscan is available for most blogging platforms and there are even automatic set-up wizards for the more popular blog providers. Installing Haloscan is relatively easy if you have even a basic knowledge of HTML.

Haloscan www.haloscan.com

▲
First impressions count: a single carefully chosen image can make a striking front page to your blog

Many blog providers offer a **word verification service** to fend off spam bots (software that creates spam automatically). However, this doesn't stop people who are paid to browse blogs, read entries, leave personalized comments, and put in a plug for a website or product. Does this system of generating unique hits make them more money? Is it an effective marketing tool? The results are still out, but what we do know is that this process is deeply annoying for bloggers.

There's no surefire way to rid yourself of the problem. What you might try is enabling selective commenting through your blog host so only members of your determined communities can leave comments. This way you'll know who's blowing up your comment box at all times, but obviously you'll also have a smaller group of potential commenters.

Sideblogs

Sideblogs are small blogs-within-blogs that are usually placed in the sidebar of a main page. Sideblogs are used in a variety of ways: providing brief thoughts on the day, relating interesting links with minimal commentary, listing favorite quotes, or displaying music

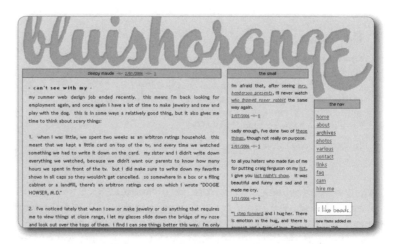

recommendations. Use them to exhibit tangential items you don't want cluttering your main posts.

Most blog hosts and systems make setting up sideblogs quite simple, and have easy-to-follow guides on how to create and incorporate them into your main template. If your blog host doesn't provide this functionality, you can go to a sideblog service, which will allow you to add a sideblog with very little effort or technical knowledge.

Sideblog www.sideblog.com

Signing up for an account with Sideblog gets you an easily updatable sideblog complete with clear installation instructions. There's no need to fiddle with your template much with this service – just add in a couple of lines of code and you're ready to go. You can edit or delete posts at any time and there are loads of display options. Free and paid versions of Sideblog are available, with the paid version giving you access to archives, comments, more customizing and display options, and syndication functionality.

User-friendly archives

Giving your readers an efficient means of navigating your old posts is a must. Blogs that feature only a single link to "previous" or "earlier" entries are annoying for anyone who wants to find something specific or browse posts relating to a specific subject. Conversely, too many links into your archives can be overwhelming.

Don't rely solely on your blog's default dating and display system as the only means of archive navigation. If a reader misses two weeks' worth of blogs, and they want to see what you were writing about back at the beginning of that stretch, they won't want to click through ten pages in succession just to get to the post they're looking for. By embedding multiple means of navigation within your posts (backlinks, categories, etc.) and within the site template or sideblog (archives, search boxes, and a directory), you will give your readers plenty of pathways to explore.

Make a best-of

When you come up with an above average post that your readers love, you may want it to be available for longer than your regular humdrum entries. But since blog posts are displayed in a reverse chronological fashion, new entries quickly bury your classics. To get around this, consider creating a "Best Of" section in your sideblog.

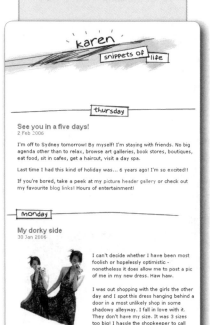

Back-link to your old posts

When posting, try to "back-link" within the text to relevant entries in the past. If you are discussing the social impact of gossip, say, then link back to your 300-word definition of gossip from two years ago. This provides context for your current thoughts, emphasizes the continuity of your blog, and encourages readers to spend some time browsing through your **archives**. Maybe they'll rediscover an entry and bring it back to light with new insight.

Clearly categorize your posts

Most blog providers let you tag each post with one or more key-words – essentially putting them into categories. A post describing a hockey match you've just seen, for example, might be tagged "sport." Then, a reader can click on the name of a category – either under an individual post or in a directory listing all the categories that you've used – to see all related posts.

Try to avoid categories that are too broad in scope, as this reduces their usefulness as a way to find specific content. Likewise, don't be too specific: you don't want to overload the reader with category choices. Pick a few categories and keep them consistent, leaving the rest in a "Miscellaneous" section.

Very basic HTML

HTML (Hyper Text Markup Language) is the most basic program-ming language used to write Web pages. HTML tells a Web browser how to display the text, images, and links on a page. It can be used to edit your text (bold, italic, sizing, colors), control your font style, create lists, and format the layout of your website. HTML also tells

History of HTML

Tim Berners-Lee invented the Web in 1989 during his time as a researcher at CERN (a meeting place for physicists from all over the world, located in Geneva, Switzerland). Berners-Lee wanted a way to organize and pool together information and files among researchers. His idea was to create links to outside references within research papers they all used. This would mean that, while reading one paper, you could quickly download another paper that held relevant text or images. Berners-Lee set about attaching addresses to his online documents, and others did the same, networking many texts together and creating a web of information.

Unfortunately, before moving forward with his plan, Berners-Lee had to invent a language that would tell computers where to go and what to do when a link was clicked – and HTML was born. Far surpassing its origins as a download director, HTML has come to be the backbone of Web design.

Some common tags

▶ **Bold** `<b></b>`

▶ **Italics** `<i></i>`

▶ **Underline** `<u></u>`

▶ **Line break** `<br>`

▶ **Horizontal rule** `<hr>`

▶ **Text size**
`<font size=4></font>`

▶ **Text color**
`<font color=red></font>`

▶ **Indented text**
`<blockquote></blockquote>`

▶ **Web link**
`<a href="www.roughguides.com">Rough Guides</a>`

▶ **Email link** `<a href="mailto:youraddress@hotmail.com">Email Me</a>`

your Web browser where to look for and insert images, as well as where links will lead. Any customization that you do to your blog will usually involve mucking around with your HTML code, adding or modifying bits and pieces of it as necessary. Luckily, HTML is easy to learn and very versatile.

HTML is based on "tags." An open tag begins an instruction, a close tag ends it; in between sits the text you want to manipulate. For example, putting the word "Blog" in between an open bold tag – **** – and a close bold tag – **** – will make the word bold on your published blog page. For example:

This in your HTML:	Will result in this on your blog:
`<b>Blog</b>`	**Blog**

With most blogging systems, you don't need to use tags to format your text – you press a bold button, say, and the bold tags will be

Tip: HTML tags are not case sensitive but most program-mers choose to write their tags in lower case.

Tip: To make a link open in a new browser window, insert this after the address: target="_blank". For example:

<a href=http://www.google. com target="_blank">Link to Google</a>

added automatically, "in the background". Still, it's good to know how HTML works, so when you want to start tinkering with your blog you'll have a better understanding of what you're looking at.

A full discussion of HTML is beyond the scope of this book, but there are plenty of good tutorials available for free online. Start here:

Web Design From Scratch www.webdesignfromscratch.com
Web Monkey www.webmonkey.com

Blogroll and other links

Adding or changing a link on your blogroll – or elsewhere on your blog – requires you to go into your **template**, identify the relevant code, and tweak or insert a bit of HTML. Here's how a link might look in your HTML:

<a href="http://www.google.com">Link to Google</a>

The URL located after the a href= is the Web address where your link points. The text between the second and third ("Link to Google") is what your reader sees and clicks on.

Manually inserting images

Most blogging systems provide an easy interface to help you upload, host, and edit images, but if you want to more precise control, or are looking to wet your toe with some simple HTML coding, you can add your images manually. Whether you want to set an image within a post, or make it a permanent fixture in a header, first upload the image to your blog's folder on whatever server you're using, and then drop the new address of the image into an IMG tag within the relevant section of your page. For example, to display the

Images as borders

As these two examples show, it's possible to create a very strong design by careful use of images as borders. But this usually requires some careful HTML work. For a start, images that appear to "wrap around" text (as in these examples) generally comprise multiple images stuck together.

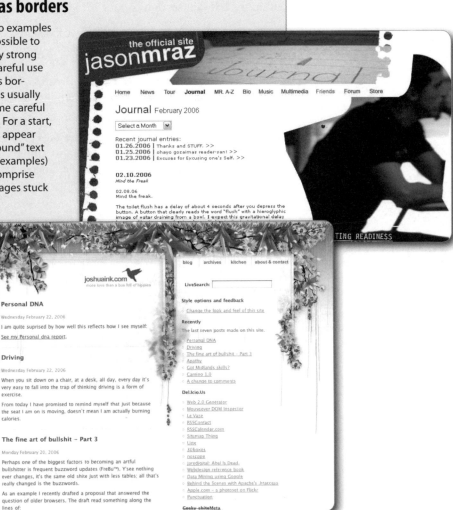

picture file **Hi_World.jpeg** within your header, you'd drop this code within the relevant section of your HTML:

```
<img src="http://www.myblog.com/Hi_World.jpeg">
```

If you want to resize and align the image, try this code:

```
<img src="http://www.image_name.jpg" hspace="3" vspace="3"
border="0" align="left" height="25%" width="25%">
```

The height and width are expressed as percentages of your total area, with the hspace, vspace, and border tags giving your picture some room round the edges. You can also choose to **align** your image to the left, right, or center of the designated area.

SUNDAY, JANUARY 08, 2006

black hawk down

a testosterone fueled bullet fest of a movie. you really have to read the book first to fully enjoy the experience i think. then you know who characters are, what's happening on-screen, what parts they left out, the entire backstory, the military training. i've read the book twice and seen the movie twice. entirely different experiences and very complementary. and what a cast: josh hartnett, ewan mcgregor, tom sizemore, william fichtner, eric bana, ron eldard, and the pre-rings orlando bloom. not a movie for everyone but certainly great for some.

11:07 PM   0 COMMENTS

Changing the height and width percentages to 50% makes the picture take up half the space of the entire blog entry, while the vspace and hspace provide a margin ▶

SUNDAY, JANUARY 08, 2006

black hawk down

a testosterone fueled bullet fest of a movie. you really have to read the book first to fully enjoy the experience i think. then you know who characters are, what's happening on-screen, what parts they left out, the entire backstory, the military training. i've read the book twice and seen the movie twice. entirely different experiences and very complementary. and what a cast: josh hartnett, ewan mcgregor, tom sizemore, william fichtner, eric bana, ron eldard, the pre-rings orlando bloom. not a movie for everyone but certainly great for some.

11:07 PM   0 COMMENTS

Loading images from other websites

You can use an image from elsewhere on the Web without copying it to your server. Simply find the address of the individual image (not the page it's displayed on) and use the IMG tag in the usual way.

Before posting an image on your blog, however, it's best to ask for permission from the copyright holder. In reality, nothing is likely to happen to you for using an image without permission – especially in the case of celebrity photos and other commonly circulated stock photos – but at the very least it's polite to ask before using, say, a drawing from an artist's website.

Tip: Before putting a file on your server, make sure its name doesn't include any spaces or unusual characters.

9 Writing tips

Once you've created a blog and made it look the way you'd like, you may secretly expect the fame and adoration to start pouring in. But unless your blog hits it big through some stroke of luck, you'll have to put in some serious effort if you want to get noticed. There are millions of blogs out there, and to stand out you'll need to develop a distinct style, good content, and an understanding (and appreciation) of your audience.

It's all about content

You probably have at least a vague idea of why you started a blog. Maybe it was to share your opinions with the world, or to keep your friends and family updated. Perhaps your company wanted a blog and it was delegated to you to start one. Or possibly your life is so unique and exciting that it would be a disservice to the public if you didn't share your every mundane detail. Whatever the reason you had for starting a blog, you may soon find yourself moving beyond your original intent.

Think about what you want your blog to become. Do you want it to be an information hub, an online expression of yourself, a platform for showcasing your skills? Whatever the case, a blog is only as strong as its content. Posts that are entertaining, informative, inspirational, humorous, or memorable will always touch a chord with readers. Here are some rules of thumb to bear in mind.

▶ **Post frequently** Blogging is about being in the now – you need to give your readers updated content on a regular basis. Even if your blog is beautifully written and designed, it will fail to keep a visitor's attention if there's nothing new to read. That said, don't post just for the sake of it (see box below).

Blogorrhea

Don't post just for the sake of posting. Make each post a directed entry that has a purpose. The classic blogorrhea post reads: "I have nothing to blog about right now, be back later." This is absolutely un-necessary; just write when you have something to say. Complaining about being bored or having nothing to write about will only make readers feel like they're wasting their time. Journal blogs are notorious for this – don't add another dull blog to the mix.

That said, even a series of profoundly boring posts blog can be amusing if done well enough:

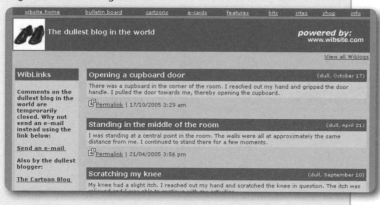

The dullest blog in the world www.wibsite.com/wiblog/dull

▶ **Life is in the details** Take the time to present some back story. Blogs aren't constrained by word length or page requirements, so explain why something is important and provide readers with some context. If another blogger has already captured a story or an opinion, link to them and use their comments to enhance your own.

▶ **Look for links that aren't already exposed** Don't automatically link to something just because everyone else has. If thousands of other bloggers have already linked to a site or story, it's hardly necessary for you to do so too – unless you can provide some additional insight or commentary. If you link to interesting items that the rest of the blogosphere has missed, your readers will value your referrals all the more.

▶ **Be brave, honest, and sexy** Blogging about the sorts of things that would have gotten you picked on in middle school can be a great way to set yourself apart from the masses. Revealing **embarrassing incidents** and exposing insecurities, emotions, and inappropriate reactions can endear you to your readership. If you are unafraid to blog some real-life issues, your readers will understand that there's an actual person behind the page, and will appreciate your willingness to let them in.

If you see it here, on Daypop Top 40 (www.daypop.com/top), chances are, it's already been linked to death
▼

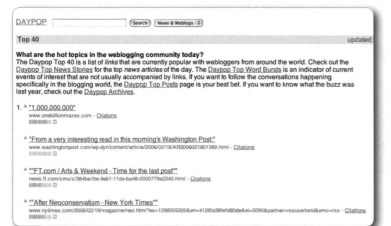

▶ **Be interesting** It sounds obvious – but personal blogs often walk the line between indulgence and comprehensiveness. Don't bore people with trivial events and encounters. Nobody cares what the lady at the grocery store looked like or how many dumbbells you lifted today … unless you can spin it to your readers in a compelling way that gives them a reason to care. Maybe the grocery store lady was later involved in a power-lifting contest?

▶ **Write for yourself** Even if you have a million visitors all eager for their daily dose of whatever it is that you serve up, keep in mind that you are still your most important reader. Blogs are supposed to be a fun and positive experience – don't let having one drag you down. Above all, entertain yourself.

Tip: TYPING WORDS IN ALL CAPS REDUCES READING SPEED BY 10%. All caps can also put readers off by giving the appearance of shouting.

Finding your voice

Blogging is by no means a sacred ritual reserved only for those able to string beautiful sentences together. Blogs are casual in tone, and what you write is generally viewed as more important than how you write. Professional writers, amateur writers, and people who are still mastering the language of their readers are all welcome on the blogosphere. Blogging is, first and foremost, about expressing yourself.

That said, writing well for blogs – with personality and energy – is an art that takes time to master, regardless of your personal style. It's important to try to find, and then cultivate, your own specific blogging voice.

To an extent, this will depend on your subject matter. Political bloggers might want to be more impersonal and academic, sticking with an informative tone and a straightforward style. **Gossip bloggers** often capture attention with pithy and entertaining comments. Journal writers who provide a lot of detail, context, and back story. If you monitor what type of writing garners the best response, you'll gain valuable tips for developing your own voice.

But whatever you're writing about, don't be afraid to let your personality shine through in your writing. If you are sarcastic and perpetually malcontent, those character traits will help make your blog stand out. If you are enthusiastic about what you're writing, if you're

Tip: Try to keep paragraphs short. The quickest way to lose readers is with giant blocks of text. Paragraph breaks give your writing room to breathe, and give readers a chance to pause and reflect before continuing.

humorous, let this shine through. Passion is contagious. Instill your words with feeling and you can create an emotional connection with your readers. If you share your loves and hates, people will get excited with you – or indignant, which is almost as good.

Be your own editor

Don't publish anything on your blog without at least reading it through. While great writing in the traditional sense isn't a requirement for a great blog, sloppy typo-ridden text will torpedo your chances of developing a decent readership.

▶ **Spelling** If you have any trouble spelling – or you're simply not careful when typing – be sure to make use of a spell check tool, as offered by most blog providers. No one minds the occasional slip, but make too many errors and your readers will start to evaporate.

▶ **Keep it snappy** For the most part, you'll want to keep your writing snappy and relevant, and free from Joyce-esque streams of consciousness. In general, if a word or sentence can be cut, then doing so will improve your post. Readers' attention spans can be short – especially online – and they'll be even shorter when people realize they are reading quantity over quality. Keeping your writing tight will drive home your point far more effectively than an impassioned diatribe full of tangential observations.

About you

People who read your blog want to know what you think, what you do, and who you are. Readers will feel closer to a blogger as they get to know the person who's writing to them, and your **About Page** should be created with this goal in mind.

Think of your About Page as the meet and greet that you'll conduct with your readers. Something as simple as "a 23-year-old woman, ex-financial services consultant, current Boston inhabitant (homesick for New York) and graduate student in science" will do. Add in "largely single, and plagued by a seemingly never-ending series of bad dates," and you quickly go from run-of-the-mill grad-schooler to a polarizing representation of unsatisfied women everywhere.

Some bloggers put a lot of thought and effort into writing a comprehensive About Page – including amusing stories, pictures, life timelines, and general likes and dislikes. Other bloggers like to provide a cast of characters (friends, family, co-workers) that are mentioned frequently in their blog. This helps new readers immediately understand that Joe is the family dog and Joey is the husband.

Then again, there's value in **remaining anonymous**. If your blog is focused on something highly titillating or potentially reputation-damaging, maybe anonymity is the way to go.

Post titles

The art of coming up with clever, humorous, informative, or catchy post titles is something that every good blogger attempts to master – and for good reason. Web posts are scanned and digested quickly, and unless you want to be ignored you need to create post titles that draw immediate attention.

Recent Posts
- One, Two
- 'I Heard He Tricked Her'
- Say My Telephone Name
- Feel Like Giving Up?
- Bazima 911

Tip: Have outbound links open up in a new browser window (see p.76). This leaves your blog open and waiting when readers return from their induced diversion.

Much like good email subjects, post titles should be used to clue in readers to your post's contents. A good email subject might be "Tentative plans for this weekend" rather than "Open me! Hurry!" Similarly, a good post title might be "Bruce Willis Marathon – Best Time Ever?" as opposed to "What I Did This Weekend … Again."

As RSS feeds, blog aggregators, and blog search engines become more popular, post titles will become ever more import (as most RSS readers will display only the post title and a snippet of the accompanying entry). People checking their newsfeeds will make their decision whether to read based solely on the strength of your post title. For more on feeds, see p.23.

Links to other sites

Many blogs operate essentially as recommendation engines, linking to new and interesting pages on the Web. Ideally, your readers will trust your opinion that a link is worth following, but people always like to have some idea of what they're about to encounter. So label or describe a link's destination – unless your intention is to shock or surprise.

The best method is to incorporate the link within a sentence that would make sense even without the link. For example, this:

> Some very cool people left our company today. They're off to work at <u>Acme Sports Company</u>.

As opposed to this:

> Some very cool people left our company today. They're off to work <u>here</u>.

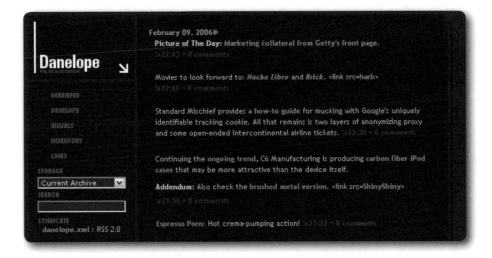

Audience-building

Picturing your typical reader – your target audience – will help you focus your blog. Readers will react to your posts, they'll be affected by your words, and they'll grow to care about your little corner of the blogosphere – but only if you keep their needs in mind.

Timing and design

If your blog presents, say, links to outrageous stories to act as a work-day diversion, then it will be important to get new posts up during working hours in the country where most of your readers are based. You'll want to have **fresh entries** ready to be read when office workers come in and fire up their computers in the morning, and you'll need to keep posting in rapid succession so your audience has a reason to return to your site every hour. Less important might be how attractive your posts look. In fact, it may be more important that your site design is neither flashy nor eye-catching – office-safe, as it were.

Stay focused

Blogs that focus on a niche tend to attract like-minded enthusiasts. A blog that meanders from personal life experiences, to cell-phone reviews, to the state of the film industry, will read more like a journal. If you want to attract a specific audience, you have to stay focused on that audience. Start separate blogs for movie news, for cell-phone reviews, and for keeping friends and family updated on your life.

Interact

Readers will be much more loyal if they feel that your blog is a two-way conversation. Make sure you offer **comments** (see p.65) and/or an **email link** (see p.66), and respond when readers leave feedback or get in touch.

Increasing traffic

10

Once you have a blog that you're ready to share, you'll need to consider just how you'll attract those throngs of adoring fans. You could sit idly by, waiting for your blog to be discovered, but chances are you'd prefer to accelerate the process. That's where promotion and marketing strategy come into play. It may seem cold and calculating to think of your blog as a product, but most of the following methods grow organically from a natural interaction with the blogosphere. It's quite likely that you'll actually enjoy promoting your blog once you see that it's not work so much as making new friends and connecting with fellow bloggers.

Measuring traffic

Before you start spreading your name around the Web, you'll want to establish some way of measuring your popularity. There are various means of doing this, but the easiest way is via a site counter. Site counters are usually free or come included in a hosted blog's feature set, and they will measure your site's visitors and referrals

increasing traffic

Tip: The paid version of Sitemeter lets you use an invisible icon – useful if you don't want anyone to know that you're tracking them.

Tip: If you're so inclined, you can turn your Sitemeter account to Private and enable password access to your traffic statistics. Look under Manager and then Privacy Level to change your level of security.

(links to your blog from other blogs or websites) over a period of a day, a week, or even an entire year. These traffic statistics will also show you exactly where your readers are, via their IP address (see p.92), what time they are coming, and even how long they stay on your page.

Sitemeter

One of the most popular site counters is Sitemeter (www.sitemeter.com), a free service offering everything you need to start stalking those who stalk you. Once signed up, simply log in to the Sitemeter website to peruse your blog's statistics. A handy graph shows you how many visitors you've had in the last day, week, month, or year.

Clicking the link to "referrals" gives you the lowdown on the individual route addresses of referrals – very useful when trying to figure out what kind of sites it would be good to nurture relationships with.

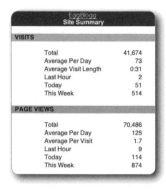

EggBlogg Site Summary	
VISITS	
Total	41,674
Average Per Day	73
Average Visit Length	0:31
Last Hour	2
Today	51
This Week	514
PAGE VIEWS	
Total	70,486
Average Per Day	125
Average Per Visit	1.7
Last Hour	9
Today	114
This Week	874

EggBlogg	
Recent Visitors by Referrals	
Detail	**Referring URL**
1	www.gardenweb.com
2	www.artnet.com
3	www.mulletjunky.com
4	www.worldbeardchampionships.com
5	www.mugshots.org
6	www.wigs.com

Other free site counters

If Sitemeter doesn't float your boat, try one of these:

Blog Patrol www.blogpatrol.com
CQ Counter cqcounter.com
WebSTAT www.nextstat.com

Visits and views

Most site counters will present you with two different categories of information: page views and visits. It's important to understand the difference. A **page view** happens every time a reader accesses a page from your blog. Since one reader might click through many pages during the course of a visit, page views are not an accurate way of counting how many readers you have.

Visits, on the other hand, are recorded only once, when someone new comes to your page. However, if the same person returns after a long enough interval (sometimes as little as 30 minutes) your site counter will consider it a separate visit. Filling the gap is the **unique visits** counter, which clocks up one notch for each computer used to visit your blog, regardless of how many times that computer is used to access the site. This gives you a pretty accurate figure,

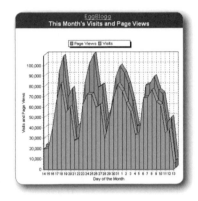

> ## Hits
>
> A very inaccurate gauge of a site's popularity, hits count every file embedded in your blog that need to load when a reader visits your site. When your page appears in a reader's Web browser, you receive one hit for the page itself, and additional hits for each piece of non-text content – images, sounds, etc. – that are uploaded. The more stuff jammed onto your page, the more hits you'll receive.

though even this isn't 100% accurate as it's based on the IP address (see below) of the computer accessing the page, and the IP address may change over time.

Using IP addresses to locate readers

Curious to find out who's visiting your blog? Every computer that connects to the Internet is issued with an **Internet Protocol** (IP) address, which represents its official location on the Internet. Each IP address comprises four sets of numbers separated by dots, such as **149.174.211.5**

Your site meter (or comments manager) will probably tell you the IP address of each of your visitors, and you can use this information to get a rough idea of where in the world each reader is located. Simply paste the addresses into an IP address locator, such as:

Geobytes www.geobytes.com/IpLocator.htm

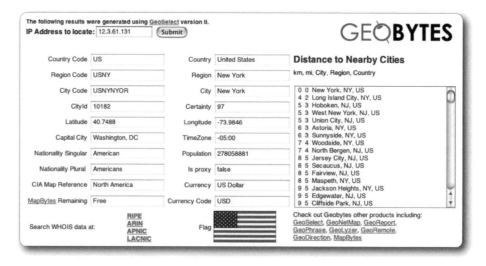

Bear in mind that basic IP address locators only tell you where the Internet service provider of each of your readers is based – not the location of the actual reader. So, for example, a reader who appears to be based in Connecticut could actually be dialling in to their ISP remotely from New York.

Tip: If for some reason, you need to remove yourself from Google, go to www.google.com/webmasters/remove.html

Get on the search engines

Search engines – and particularly Google – are the default method for finding information online. Naturally, then, it's important to make sure that all the major search engines can find your blog – and preferably "rate" it highly so that it comes close to the top of the results lists for relevant searches.

Search engines work by automatically following links on websites ("spidering") and creating a snapshot of each page they find. So, as long as there are links coming in and out of your site, the search engines should find you eventually. But you may as well manually submit your blog address to the bigger search engines:

Google www.google.com/addurl.html
Yahoo submit.search.yahoo.com

Within a day or two of submitting your blog, all of your entries and archives will be searchable via the Web. This doesn't mean that you'll suddenly attract thousands of visitors; it simply means that you're now one of the millions of stars in a particular search engine's sky.

Add your URL to Google

Share your place on the net with us.

We add and update new sites to our index each time we crawl the web, and we invite you to submit your URL here. We do not add all submitted URLs to our index, and we cannot make any predictions or guarantees about when or if they will appear.

Please enter your full URL, including the http:// prefix. For example: http://www.google.com/. You may also add comments or keywords that describe the content of your page. These are used only for our information and do not affect how your page is indexed or used by Google.

Please note: Only the top-level page from a host is necessary; you do not need to submit each individual page. Our crawler, Googlebot, will be able to find the rest. Google updates its index on a regular basis, so updated or outdated link submissions are not necessary. Dead links will 'fade out' of our index on our next crawl when we update our entire index.

URL:

Comments:

Optional: To help us distinguish between sites submitted by individuals and those automatically entered by software robots, please type the squiggly letters shown here into the box below.

mented

(Add URL)

Raise your ranking

Raising your ranking on Google and other search engines is a dark art that keeps some people in full-time employment. There isn't space here to go into too much detail, but the single most important thing to know is that the order of Google results is largely based on the number of sites linking to each of results.

This approach – called **PageRank** – works on the premise that the more interesting and useful a page is, the more people will link to

Google bombing

Bloggers sometimes use their collective linking power to have some fun at Google's expense. If they make a concentrated effort to point to a particular site in great numbers, all using the same link text, they can dictate the top Google results for a particular search phrase. This technique has come to be known as Google bombing.

One of the first instances of Google bombing was undertaken by Adam Mathes. After identifying Google's PageRank parameters, he set out to make any searches for "talentless hack" bring up his friend Andy's website. With the help of a "Google bombing army," who linked to Andy's site with specific keywords, Adam's Google bomb worked – and Andy was doused in the stink of the exceedingly ordinary.

Since then, Google bombs have been used by bloggers for various humorous reasons, such as linking searches for "miserable failure" to George W. Bush's official website. Many websites and businesses have attempted, with varying success, to use the same strategies to drive up their own PageRank.

A google bomb on the term "miserable failure"

it. The clever bit is that Google also considers which sites are doing the linking, and weights the value of the link according to its own PageRank rating. So a link from a popular site will count more toward your rating than a link from an unknown blog.

In short, then, the best way to raise your ranking on Google (and indeed most search engines) is to impress bloggers and website owners – preferably popular ones – to link to you. Following are some tactics for doing just this.

Pulling in links

As if by gravitational attraction (or perhaps as a means of protection), bloggers tend to group together, forming online circles of friends that are constantly expanding. These circles are your most basic promotional tool: as you develop your circle, you're simultaneously opening up a wider audience for your blog and expanding your potential fanbase. Word-of-mouth aside, even the most basic of blogs will have a blogroll (see box), or will link to favored

blogroll
- alex
- alvin
- anna
- ariel
- cat
- chrissy
- connie
- cougar
- eric a
- eric d
- eric g
- fingers
- gene
- guiao

The blogroll

A blogroll is simply a list of links to recommended blogs maintained in a specific section of your blog (usually in a sidebar). Depending on your camp, the term derives either from its cross-linking functions (US) or from its toilet-tissue-like qualities, with a nod to the suspected value within these sorts of lists (UK).

places within their posts. It won't take much to expand beyond your immediate circle of friends.

Use the comments box

As already discussed (see p.70), **comments** can often lead to group conversation that draws readers back time and again. Besides maintaining your own comments box, you should explore those on other people's blogs. By cleverly or sympathetically commenting on someone else's post, you may just receive some visits in return, or even be added to a blogroll.

Link and blogroll etiquette

You can hasten your discovery by other bloggers by engaging in a game of link reciprocity. Most bloggers are fastidious about checking their site referrals, and once they notice an unknown blog sending hits their way, they're very likely to check it out. If they like what they see, they might place your blog on their own blogroll. And just like that, you have the chance to impress an entirely new set of readers.

Many bloggers take the line of **blogrolling** whoever blogrolls them purely as a courtesy. Other bloggers will only link to blogs that they actually admire – a policy which can at times be seen as rude. However, because blogrolls can get to be quite large, there's nothing particularly discourteous about the latter practice. Your blogroll is a reflection of your personal taste, and too many boring blogs will make you seem boring as well. Adding blogs to your blogroll is akin to recommending movies or books to friends – make your opinion matter.

Syndicate your site via RSS

How can you let your regular readers know when you've updated your blog? The best way is to set it up with an **RSS feed** (see p.23). Most major blog hosts make this very easy. If you're using Blogger, for example, go to Settings and then Site Feed, decide if you want to upload the full text of each post or an excerpted version, and that's it – your blog now has a feed.

If your blog host doesn't provide you with an easy way to create an RSS feed, the following online tutorial will help you set one up. Be warned that will involve some coding knowledge, so may not be suitable for everyone.

Making An RSS Feed www.searchenginewatch.com/sereport/article.php/2175271

Once your feed is ready to go, consider the widely used services of FeedBurner, which promises to help you "build awareness, track circulation, and implement revenue-generating programs in your feed."

FeedBurner www.feedburner.com

Finally, be sure to promote your RSS feed. Link to it on your blog and submit it to third-party directories such as those found here:

RSS Submission www.rss-specifications.com/rss-submission.htm

Get your name known

A few final tips for upping your presence in the blogosphere:

▶ **Join a blog ring** These community portals (see p.21) can be a quick way to get your blog onto the monitors of interested parties, offering you a ready-made audience likely to be more interested in your blog than is the random Web surfer. Can't find a suitable ring? Consider starting up your own.

▶ **Get listed** A blog portal, or directory, is essentially the same thing but on a grander scale and without the personal touch. Most arrange thousands of blogs into categories, but some focus on a specific subject area. Beyond massive sites like Google, there are a number of refined directories more suited to your needs (see p.20):

▶ **Get reviewed** Once you have some entries worth reading and a blog that you can be proud of, you can submit it for review at one of the various weblog review sites (see p.19). These sites can be a fun and exciting – or soul-destroying – way to receive feedback on your work.

▶ **Enter for awards** Winning a blog award (see p.17) is not like winning an Oscar, with gala dinner and red carpet, but it will gain you serious respect in the blogosphere and drive up your readership. Even if you don't win, submitting your blog or being nominated for an award may create welcome exposure.

Money, money, money

11

While there are a growing number of bloggers finding gold at the end of the rainbow, the truth of the matter is that 99% of bloggers will never make a cent. The numbers of professional bloggers are very few and financial success is rare (and often fleeting). Bloggers may aspire to many things, but more often than not blogs are simply hobbies.

But that doesn't mean that you can't try to make a little cash – for example, to cover the operating costs of your blog (which can shoot up if it gets too popular). As this chapter explains, it's easy to ask for donations, offer advertisements, sell merchandise, and join **Amazon's Associates** progam. Unless you have a huge readership, you'd be lucky to raise $50 a month in total, but something's better than nothing.

Another approach is to focus on developing a reputation as a brilliant blog writer and hope to get picked up by a publisher (see p.107) or an established multi-author blog (see p.103).

Donations

The most straightforward way to make money from your blog is to solicit donations from your readers. Some bloggers ask for contributions of a dollar or two a month to help cover costs. Others just ask for donations when times are tough, creating pledge drives to help them pay rent, Internet bills, or credit card interest.

Kottke.org

In the early part of 2005, **Jason Kottke**, owner of one the most popular personal blogs, www.kottke.org, decided to quit his day job and turn professional blogger for one year. His new job sees him supported entirely by his readers – 25,000 daily, by his estimates. While Kottke certainly wasn't the first or only person to try to make his living by blogging, he holds a position as one of the Web's most influential bloggers, and his decision to turn pro has sent ripples through the blogosphere.

Kottke's blog doesn't offer any form of service or product. Neither does it offer advertising space, or any sort of commercial way to make money using the Web. Instead, like those very first blogs that came into existence, kottke.org is just all about Jason – what Jason likes, what Jason thinks, what Jason does each day. He's modeled his decision to make money and live off a non-topical or business-orientated blog as a social and economic experiment.

On February 22, 2006, Jason revealed that roughly 1,450 **micropatrons** had donated $39,900 over the course of his one-year experiment.

Doing kottke.org as a full-time job

posted February 22, 2005 at 09:04 am

I recently quit my web design gig and -- as of today -- will be working on kottke.org as my full-time job. And I need your help.

I'm asking the regular readers of kottke.org (that's you!) to become micropatrons of kottke.org by contributing a moderate sum of money to help enable me to edit/write/design/code the site for one year on a full-time basis. If you find kottke.org valuable in any way, please consider giving whatever you feel is appropriate.

This will be a one-time "fund drive" lasting 3 weeks, you may make contributions via PayPal, credit card, or check, there will be some great gifts as an incentive for you to give (more details here), and your contributions will be the primary means of support for the site. And yes, I have absolutely no idea if this will work and I'm completely nervous and exhilarated by the challenges ahead.

Support kottke.org by becoming a micropatron today...

Contribute* »»

Give $30 or more and you could procure a great thank you gift for yourself. Details inside...

* PayPal, Visa, Mastercard, Discover, AmEx, and personal checks accepted.

Whatever your approach, you may find that your blog host offers a "tip jar" tool linked directly to a PayPal account (see box). In a similar vein, Amazon Wishlists are popular with bloggers who think their readers might buy them gifts from time to time.

PayPal

PayPal (www.paypal.com) has overwhelmed all other forms of online currency exchange to become the standard for transferring cash over the Internet. And if you have a credit card and an email account, it's easy to link your tip jar to your PayPal account (this arrangement may in fact be the default set-up your blog host provides). Blog donations don't usually crack the dollar mark, but luckily PayPal lets users send money in amounts as little as a few cents. You can also use PayPal as an online cash register for any item you might hawk on your blog – from T-shirts with your site's slogan to coffee mugs and stress balls.

American Express Card

We accept the American Express card. (To use Visa or MasterCard, choose the PayPal option below.) Fill in the amount of your donation, click the button, and you'll be whisked to a secure Amex server where you enter credit card info.

| 0.00 |

AMERICAN EXPRESS | Click to Contribute

Visa/Mastercard via PayPal

We accept Visa and Mastercard via PayPal. Click the credit card icon to enter PayPal's secure site, and fill in your donation info.

PayPal DONATE | VISA DONATE

In the Mail

If you'd rather just send cash, check, or money order through the mail for any amount large or small, our mailing address is:

AndrewSullivan.com
8210 W 4th Street
Los Angeles CA 90048

Please make checks payable to asdotcom LLC.

Merchandising

If you have a popular blog with an appealing logo or message, you could try selling merchandise. With a service such a **CafePress**, it's amazingly easy to emblazon your catchphrases and logo onto everything from sweatshirts and coffee mugs to light-switch covers.

CafePress creates items on demand, eliminating the headache of having to stock merchandise in anticipation of sales that may never materialize. They also handle all the admin of shipping and billing needs. Again, you're unlikely to make your fortune, but a few dozen T-shirts a month to loyal readers might be enough to put you in the black.

CafePress www.cafepress.com

Advertising

From pop-ups to banners, advertising is everywhere on the Web, so why shouldn't you have a taste of the action? The ideal way to make money from advertisements is to host ads in direct agreement with a company or corporation. However, most blogs lack the sort of readership that would entice a company into this kind of arrangement. And if you don't have Budweiser or Nike knocking on your door, then you'll need a program to help do the leg work for you. As with so many areas of online life, the market is dominated by Google…

Google AdSense

Google's AdSense (www.google.com/adsense) is a service that provides unobtrusive advertising on your site based on the contents of each page. Write a post about the new digital camera you bought, for example, and AdSense will offer up ads for consumer electronics on your blogs. Readers will, hopefully, click on these ads and, with each click, earn you some money. The income won't be huge (the exact value of each click varies according to a keyword bidding system), but there are no upfront costs so there's no harm in trying the system out.

Some blogs are tailor-made for a program like AdSense. Product blogs, hobby blogs, and **niche blogs** usually attract a following of educated, cross-clicking consumers who are relatively likely to follow ads directing them to specific products. AdSense also provides a Google search box for your visitors, and, each time it's used in combination with a follow-up click on an ad in the results, you get paid.

AdBrite www.adbrite.com

With AdBrite, you can buy or sell advertising space on blogs and websites. If you have ads to sell, AdBrite will let you know where you can place them, for how long, and for how much. If you have space to sell, just let AdBrite know what you're offering, how much you charge, and which ads you'll accept.

Blogads www.blogads.com

Blogads is a service that matches advertisers and bloggers. Once you register, advertisers (generally small companies or individuals) choose you, and then you either accept or deny their patronage depending on your personal convictions. Running Blogads on your site is free, but the service keeps a percentage of your earnings.

Commission Junction www.cj.com

Commission Junction gives bloggers the ability to partner with thousands of advertisers. Payouts differ by advertiser, and users can choose to partner with as many advertisers as they wish.

Amazon Associates

Amazon's Associates program allows any website to try and make money by pointing readers to books, DVDs, and other products on sale at the online retail giant. When you sign up, you get a unique link code, which you then use when creating each link to Amazon. If someone follows the link and buys the product, the tracking code is enabled and you will get a percentage of the sale price – between 4% and 10% – from Amazon. It's good practice to use the Amazon Associates program any time you refer to a book, movie, or album on your blog, for example, on your "Currently Reading" or "Currently Watching" lists. For more information, see: www.amazon.com/associates

Writing for others

If the thought of trying to make money from your own blog makes you break out in hives, why not reduce your personal risk by blogging for someone else? Two of the bigger blog conglomerates, **Gawker Media** and **Weblogs, Inc.**, hire writers to post entries for their websites. Gawker Media publishes fifteen themed blogs, and Weblogs, Inc. publishes around eighty.

Blogging at work: Don't get Dooced!

It can take years to become a professional blogger, so in the meantime it's important not to lose the day job. Just like Web surfing and instant messaging, blogging has become common in many offices. But if you do blog at work, bear in mind that your employer may find out. And because blog posts record and display the time they were created, an employer can easily determine that you were slacking in office hours, which might result in a slap on the wrist.

More importantly, tread extremely carefully when writing about – or displaying pictures of – anything to do with your company and colleagues. Many bloggers have been fired for just this. Delta Airlines suspended a stewardess, for example, for posting pictures of herself in uniform while posing on board an empty plane. The pictures weren't risqué or offensive, but Delta considered them "inappropriate" and terminated her contract.

Queen of Sky queenofsky.journalspace.com
I Hate Queen of Sky ihatequeenofsky.journalspace.com

Heather B. Armstrong, proprietor of the blog Dooce, was the first famous case of a fired blogger. In February 2002, an anonymous co-worker emailed vice presidents of her company to inform them that Heather had written unsavory things about them on her weblog. Soon after, she was sacked, leading to the coinage of the term "dooced" to refer to anyone fired due to their blog.

Dooce www.dooce.com

CELEBRATING FIVE YEARS OF PUBLIC STUPIDITY
february 2006

In another infamous case, Jessica Cutler, "The Washingtonienne", was fired from her post as assistant to Senator Mike DeWine in 2004 for blogging about sexual exploits with highly placed government staffers. She used her blog to share her stories and to brag to friends about the amount of money that she would sometimes collect from her sexual dalliances. Popular Washington, DC gossip site Wonkette linked to Cutler's blog, and, despite Cutler's best efforts to take down the two-week-old blog, bosses saw her writing and immediately fired her. Since then, Cutler has achieved minor celebrity for her (mis)deeds. The blog's archives are still available via:

The Washingtonienne washingtoniennearchive.blogspot.com

Another high-profile case, in October 2003, saw Michael Hanscom (pictured), a temp worker at Microsoft, fired for posting pictures of Apple Macintosh G5s on a Microsoft loading dock.

Michael Hanscom
www.michaelhanscom.com/
eclecticism

Despite all this, blogging negative things about the workplace can also have a positive effect. Electronic Arts, the largest video game studio in the world, recently changed their overtime policies after a blog post by an employee's wife. The blog criticized the long, uncompensated, additional hours that her husband had to work on a year-round basis, and resulted in a class-action lawsuit against EA. EA lost and had to pay $15.6 million in backpay and compensation. For the full story, see:

EA Spouse ea-spouse.livejournal.com

Writers for these blogs can be paid anywhere between $500 and $3,000 a month, depending (as with most jobs) on experience and expertise. If you're employed by Gawker, they'll require somewhere in the neighborhood of a dozen posts per day, with each averaging between 100 and 200 words. As a point of comparison, the pay rate per word for a blogger and a typical US freelance print journalist is $0.05 and $1.50, respectively.

Gawker Media www.gawker.com
Gawker Media, founded by Nick Denton, publishes a growing network of popular blogs, including Gawker (NYC gossip), Defamer (Hollywood gossip), Wonkette (DC gossip), and Gizmodo (gadgets).

Weblogs, Inc. www.weblogsinc.com
Weblogs, Inc., a blog conglomerate focusing mostly on technology, media, and sciences, employs about 150 bloggers and is said to have revenues of $1 million annually from Google's AdSense alone. In 2005 it was sold to AOL for an estimated $20–30 million dollars.

While getting hired as a professional blogger isn't exactly lucrative, blogging for someone else can get you noticed. While the short-term benefits may not be equal to the amount of effort you put in, the long-term benefits may well be worth the struggle. **Volunteering** your services to an up-and-coming blog may turn into a paid gig if the blog starts to achieve some revenue. And, if you're good enough, blogging for a high-profile site can lead to a paid position in traditional media, or open the doors to any number of opportunities. At the very least, blogging will give you writing experience and an opportunity to have your work noticed.

Get published

Bloggers are increasingly picked up by book publishers for their built-in audiences and unique perspectives. Wil Wheaton, one of the highest-profile bloggers, received a three-book deal based in no small part on the strength of his blog's fan-base. Salam Pax, the famous Iraqi blogger, sold a book that was basically his blog pressed between a front and back cover. Julia Powell decided to cook all 524 recipes in Julia Child's *Mastering the Art of French Cooking* as part of a re-examination of her life. She blogged the experience, and her online journey is now available in book form. Belle de Jour, the blog of a call girl in London, launched a book. Jessica Cutler, the infamous Washingtonienne, who blogged for a mere two weeks about her sexual escapades on Capitol Hill, also has a book.

Some of these book deals are even rewarding bloggers with instant riches. Stephanie Klein, heroine of the personal blog **Greek Tragedy**, has a six-figure, two-book deal. If you write a well-received blog that has a sizable audience, a book deal may be in your future too.

Even if you can't snag an immediate book deal, many newspapers and magazines are hiring bloggers to create content for their online and print publications. Some bloggers score weekly columns on a major news site like ESPN.com; some bloggers write daily slice-of-life editorials for their local newspaper. Blogs are helping people tell stories, so it only makes sense that these online stories, and authors, are finding their way into traditional media outlets.

Elizabeth Spiers

The original blogger on Gawker was Elizabeth Spiers, an independent equity analyst who maintained a personal blog in her spare time. Spiers' snarky commentary on New York media life soon gained her, and Gawker, many fans. Despite becoming almost synonymous with the brand, she jumped ship less than a year later to take a job as a contributing writer and editor at *New York Magazine* – the first example of someone using blogging as springboard to a high-profile media position. Spiers later became Editor in Chief of Mediabistro, a creative industries' website, and is now working on a book.

What's out there ?

Journals & interests

12

As should be clear by now, blogs come in all shapes and sizes, and serve all sorts of functions. This chapter takes a deeper look at some of the most popular blog categories, from hobbies to technology. Blogging's growing role in politics, journalism, education and business are dealt with in chapters 13–16.

Journal blogs

Writing is therapeutic, and the need to express life's frustrations and joys on the page is an age-old tradition harkening back to the earliest days of quill and ink. Of course, bloggers who choose to lay their lives on the page are effectively exposing themselves to anyone with an Internet connection. While most of these journals are ignored, it is possible for just about anyone to find such a blog – even ridiculed bosses and jilted ex-lovers – with relative ease.

Safety and security concerns aside, journal blogs can be some of the most revealing and intriguing blogs around. Reading another person's journal can be pure voyeurism, or an interesting insight into lives very different from your own.

Building communities

Many bloggers write for an audience of one, even if they happen to receive attention from thousands. Blogging offers people a chance to express themselves, whether manifested as words, pictures, music, drawings, or some combination of the above. Self-expression leads to sharing, and, from there, a community forms. These communities might consist of a group of friends who traffic in personal updates and interpersonal gossip, or a group of hobbyists searching out fellow enthusiasts on the Internet.

Blogs typically start with a few brief posts and a list of links kept for personal convenience. As people connect to one another, they share their links and generate additional posts and comments around common topics. Soon, a circle of readers revolves around the blog, and as individual blog circles start to overlap with one another (at an exponential rate) they create sprawling but interlinked communities. From simple self-expression to massively interconnected blogosphere, that's the path bloggers have traveled toward connecting, supporting, and entertaining people.

East/West eastwest.blogspot.com
Blogging communities might consist of a mere duo using journals to keep in touch with each other, like the authors of the now defunct East Coast/West Coast journal blog. Choire, located in New York, and Philo, living in San Francisco, started East/West to stay tied together despite the physical distance separating them. They blogged independently of each other but shared the same blog space, separated by two columns on one page. Their daily writings made for great reading and their different writing styles complemented each other perfectly, making East West quite a popular destination in the early days of blogging.

NYC Bloggers www.nycbloggers.com

New York is home to millions of bloggers, and this site organizes over 6,000 of them by subway stop. Started by two bloggers who wanted a way to share the thrill of reading, and meeting, fellow bloggers in their neighborhoods. Regional and country lists of bloggers were always available, but by organizing their list using subway stops NYC Bloggers had a (then unique) visual flair for their site.

Blog Meetup blog.meetup.com

Naturally, some bloggers that met online wanted to meet offline. Blog Meetup was started with the idea of connecting local bloggers. By entering in an area code, users can find the monthly (or more frequent) blogger meet-ups that are being organized in their area. The Blog Meetup website displays the largest blogger meet-up groups as well as the newest ones.

SXSW Conference www.sxsw.com

The South By Southwest Music and Media Conference is in its twentieth year and takes place in Austin, Texas. Its Interactive Festival has traditionally brought together geeks, tech entrepreneurs, and digital innovators from around the world for a week's worth of keynote speeches.

The SXSW Conference has served as the de facto blogger conference. The Bloggie Awards are presented here and many bloggers are asked to present and speak on panels. As blogging has grown, the number of bloggers who flock to SXSW to socialize and discuss blogging matters has increased exponentially.

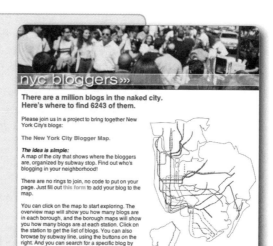

nyc bloggers »

There are a million blogs in the naked city. Here's where to find 6243 of them.

Please join us in a project to bring together New York City's blogs:

The New York City Blogger Map.

The idea is simple:
A map of the city that shows where the bloggers are, organized by subway stop. Find out who's blogging in your neighborhood!

There are no rings to join, no code to put on your page. Just fill out this form to add your blog to the map.

You can click on the map to start exploring. The overview map will show you how many blogs are in each borough, and the borough maps will show you how many blogs are at each station. Click on the station to get the list of blogs. You can also browse by subway line, using the buttons on the right. And you can search for a specific blog by name using the search feature.

That said, many journal blogs are painfully boring and mundane – what someone had for dinner, how many reps they took at the gym, the number of friends that called them today, and, all too often, what their pet has been up to recently. It's enough to get some people quite annoyed:

Why Web Journals Suck www.nobody-knows-anything.com/websuck.html
I Hate Weblogs mama.indstate.edu/users/bones/WhyIHateWebLogs.html

Ultimately, it all comes down to whether someone has an interesting life, interesting angles or insights, or an interesting turn of phrase. So, while a blog focusing on a cat has great potential for being dull, it can also be quite brilliant:

Stuff On My Cat www.stuffonmycat.com
A photoblog of cats with stuff put on them. Cats in costume, cats lost amidst a pile of toys, cats everywhere.

Following are some other popular journal blogs, between them showing the wide range of the genre.

Bazima www.bazima.com/hello.htm
Freelance writer and graphic designer Blaise K's take on dating in New York City, written with attitude, honesty, and self-effacing humor.

The Collar Purple www.collarpurple.com
This site is dedicated to the S&M and spanking enthusiast. Posts chronicle Boss' dungeon adventures, however taboo they may be.

Christian-Mother.com www.christian-mother.com
An online forum where worrisome mothers collectively design conversion schemes for their heathen children.

Little Yellow Different www.littleyellowdifferent.com
Ernie Hsiung has earned quite a devoted following, and numerous blog awards, for his humorous posts detailing his life as an Asian-American (gay)

man, a freelance and sometimes-out-of-work programmer, and a general nerd at heart. Ernie is unafraid to let his personality shine through in his blog and uses engaging stories, pictures, and a self-deprecating style to capture the imagination and attention of his readers. Ernie's weblog is the prototypical personal, journal-style, blog. While LYD may not receive much mainstream attention, or directly impact the future of our world, it has made Ernie a star in the blogosphere.

Weblog Wannabe www.wannabegirl.org
A winner of several Bloggie Awards since its inception in 2000, Weblog Wannabe chronicles the adventures of Canadian Firda and her family. Filled with cool links, engaging stories, a daily haiku, and photos.

Privacy matters

If you start your own journal blog, consider adopting a pseudonym – and avoid specifying your address and day-to-day schedules. Stalking, buglary, harassment, and identity theft are all unlikely, but there's no point exposing yourself to unnecessary risks. Also consider using fake names for friends and family who pop up in your posts – for the sake of their privacy, and to avoid negative comments on colleagues and acquaintances backfiring.

Professional blogs

Professional blogs give laypeople a insider's view of high-paying, high-stress careers in medicine, law, finance, and the like. Future doctors blogging from medical schools are especially engaging – it's hard not to be drawn into someone's first reaction to a cadaver, or the description of an emotionally tense revelation of life-threatening news.

Some off-the-beaten path professions have also spawned popular and widely read blogs – from big-game fishing and freelance writing to the entertainment industry. One particularly successful example was **Belle de Jour** (see p.107), penned by an anonymous London call girl (supposedly) who would write about her various customers and the personas she would adopt during their time together.

While many professional blogs read like journals, others are designed to give advice and share expertise with the general public, and have a strong focus on interaction between readers and writers. Such blogs cover subjects ranging from buying and selling real estate (see p.153) to coping with cancer.

Nee Naw www.neenaw.co.uk
Mike Myers, of the **London Ambulance Service**, blogs his rise from dispatcher to (eventual) paramedic. He takes the time to teach the general public a little bit about how, when, and why to call for an ambulance. Myers' stories are often humorous in nature, making for an engaging and informative read.

ShoutFish www.shoutfish.com
If you love fly fishing, this is your promised land. ShoutFish is up on all manner of fishing news, and provides links to other great resources like upcoming events, tournaments, and even Podcasts. A great place to tell your "one that got away" story.

The Cancer Blog www.thecancerblog.com
Very informative blog that catalogues and organizes worldwide news regarding cancer and related medical topics. Every form of the disease is covered, and everyone is encouraged to share their stories.

Fantasy blogs

Some people use their blogs to co-opt the identity of fictional characters or celebrities, and plenty of people tune into such sites for a chuckle or two. Commonly referred to as fantasy blogs, these sites are penned by anonymous writers impersonating superstars such as Britney Spears – or, even stranger, Britney Spears' unborn fetus.

Fetus Spears www.liquidgeneration.com/blog/fetusblog/blogger.html

Politicians are habitually mocked in the same way, with disgruntled constituents turning to blogging to castigate their policies and personalities.

The President's Blog presidentgeorgebush.blogspot.com
Dubya's faux journal lets you finally get inside his head. Don't worry: there's plenty of space.

the president's blog

A SAFE ENVIRONMENT WHERE I, THE PRESIDENT OF THE UNITED STATES, CAN FREELY EXPRESS MY OPINIONS, EMOTIONS AND LIFE WITH THE INTERNET.

At the other end of the fantasy blog spectrum lie fictional characters brought to life by obsessive fans. The Very Secret Diaries, for example, chronicled the thoughts of *Lord Of The Rings*' favorite elf as he undertook the task of overthrowing the evil Sauron. Readers were given a look into Legolas' constant preening and posturing. A sample entry reads: "Am definitely prettiest member of the Fellowship. Go me! Far too dark in Mines of Moria to brush hair properly. Am very afraid I am developing a tangle."

The Very Secret Diaries www.ealasaid.com/misc/vsd

Hobby blogs

Hobby blogs can take one of two forms. The first type details a journey of the hobbyist – weekly updates, say, on the rebuilding of an '84 T-Bird. As posts are uploaded, people can leave suggestions, or even announce that they have the rare spare part needed for the authentic grill plate. Within this genre, cars are popular…

Classic Mini Madness h8bmwmini.blogspot.com
The motoring experience of one fan's classic Mini Cooper. Includes frequent news updates on all things Mini.

The Money Pit classicmotoring.blogspot.com
The ongoing saga of UK resident Greg Harvey's frustrating, yet rewarding, attempts at keeping two classic cars on the road: a 1974 Lotus Elan and a 1971 Fiat 500 Berlina F.

…but there are plenty of other examples. Bloggers have undertaken to cook every recipe in a Julia Child cookbook, for example, or to play one year of professional poker. One professional writer even took it upon himself to see how much he could make by playing the video game **Ultima Online** over the course of twleve months.

Play Money www.juliandibbell.com/playmoney
Ultima Online is a MMORPG (massive multiplayer online role-playing game) for which many players buy and sell virtual items – from golden ingots to shards of land – on eBay. Intrigued by this real market for imaginary items, writer Julian Dibbell wanted to see if he could make this hobby a viable source of income, and documented his experiment every step of the way. He ended up making a small profit collecting, and has even published a book on the experiment.

The other type of hobby blog is one that simply collects news and information about a particular pastime. If collecting comics is a passion of yours, you might read a comic-book blog to keep up on industry trends and artist news. Even obscure hobbies like the collection and admiration of wooden pencils have their place in the blogosphere.

Pencil Revolution www.pencilrevolution.com
For the pencil enthusiast inside everyone. Aficionados of wood, graphite, and rubber come together to discuss the finer points.

Tech blogs

Geeks invented the Internet, and they invented blogging. So there's little wonder that a decent chunk of the blogosphere is devoted to technical matters – **software**, **hardware**, and other wares. Aside from all-encompassing sites such as Slashdot, Kuro5hin, and Techdirt, there are also thousands of blogs focused on more specific subjects, from open-source Web browsers to the art of XTML.

Slashdot www.slashdot.org
This venerable site distributes tech news around the clock. Though it doesn't describe itself as a blog, it has a very blog-like structure, with posts and comments exhaustively dissecting all kinds of techie developments. When Slashdot links to a story, the number of readers following the link can number in the tens of thousands – a barrage of traffic that can easily cause smaller sites to crash. This process of traffic-induced seizure has been deemed the "slashdot effect," though any hugely popular blog can have the same effect.

Techdirt www.techdirt.com
Commentary on the latest technology and finance news. There's an enhanced professional version for corporate use.

Kuro5hin www.kuro5hin.org
Examines the way technological advances influence with culture, media, politics, science, and the arts.

One popular subset of tech blogs is the **gadget blog** – entire sites devoted to laptops, PDAs, mobile phones, MP3 players, digital cameras, and other gizmos. Big-name sites like Gizmodo and Engadget (see p.186) are even sent prototypes and soon-to-be unveiled products for review.

Gadget Review www.gadgetreview.com
Everything from new MP3-player reviews to advice on where to buy astronautical glass Aerogel.

Celebrity blogs

Newsstands are filled with publications devoted to celebrities and their alternately fabulous and mundane lives, and the blogosphere is no different. There are celebrity blogs focusing on subsets of stars – the Frat Pack, Dualstar, etc. – and others that adhere to some overarching theme, from under-25 blonds to friends of Kate Moss. Celebrity stalking is a common feature of posts, with readers submitting hastily snapped pictures or slightly embellished stories involving Hollywood-style shenanigans.

Just Jared www.justjared.com
Started by a college student fascinated with Paris Hilton's escapades, Just Jared soon expanded to cover celebrity gossip and has become one of Hollywood's top gossip sites.

It's not just commoners blogging about stars' lives, of course. The rich and famous have started taking to the blogosphere themselves. In the beginning, it was C-level names like Wil Wheaton (see p.11) and Dave Barry, but many bigger stars have since jumped on the blogwagon. To pick just two examples…

Moby www.moby.com/journal
Moby maintains a frank personal journal, stripping away any perceived glamour of his life as a celebrity musician.

Margaret Cho www.margaretcho.net/blog
Comedienne and actress Margaret Cho uses her blog to post long entries about everything from politics and music to her new tattoo.

Certain types of celebrities are almost *required* to start blogs. **Reality TV** show contestants are probably number one in this demographic, as blogs from contestants of nearly every season of shows like *The Real World*, *Big Brother*, *Survivor*, *American/Pop Idol*, and *The Bachelorette* have shown.

The Real World/Road Rules Blog
realworldroadrules.blogspot.com
Need to know what your favorite
MTV reality stars are up to? This is the blog

for you. Also includes links to cast members' individual blogs.

American Idol Blog american.idolblog.com
Keeping readers updated on the latest news from America's number one show, this blog includes video and audio of the most recent performances by each aspiring idol.

Some bloggers have even reinvented the reality genre especially for the blogosphere. **Reality blog games** typically follow the format of one of the major TV shows (*Big Brother*, *Puppetmaster* and *Blind Date*, to give three examples), though so far they've all been unofficial, with no link to the relevant TV station.

Survivor Blog survivor.mu.nu

One of the first reality blog games (conducted in 2001), took its lead from the hit television show *Survivor*. Twelve people took turns posting on a group blog and the Internet audience voted contestants off one by one, until a final survivor emerged to claim the grand prize – a year's worth of Web hosting and minimal cash.

Sports blogs

Sports fans are known for their fanaticism, obsessing over coverage of their team in newspapers, magazines, and cable channels. The emergence of the Internet added a drip feed of statistics, injury reports, trade deals, coaching shifts, roster changes, and real-time updates. Then came blogs – from fans, from teams, and even from individual sports stars, tracking life on the road and emotions after wins and losses.

Paul Shirley's ESPN Blog www.nba.com/suns/news/shirley_blog.html

While not technically a blog, pro basketball player Paul Shirley's writings for ESPN.com follow his journey from benchwarmer for the Phoenix Suns in 2005 to his recent foray into the minor leagues of baseball.

Paul Shirley's Road Ramblings

You know Paul Shirley. He's that tall, thin-looking lad you see in the lay-up line during pre-game warm-ups at AWA. The one that sits at the end of the bench cheering on all your favorite Suns and doling out high-fives during timeouts. Yes, he's got the best seat in the house, but Shirley's much more than your typical 12th man. He's now an up-and-coming author.

The 27-year-old forward -- who made the club's opening day roster, was cut before the opening game, but then re-signed in January -- kept an online diary for Suns.com during the team's five-game road trip in mid-March. A diary that caused quite the stir among media members, who were equally surprised and entertained by his unique and honest insight into life in the NBA. Shirley's daily blog was mentioned on ESPN's "Cold Pizza" and on ESPN.com, and was covered in several newspapers around the country, including USA Today.

♦ **Video:** Paul Unplugged
♦ **More:** Paul on the Playoffs

Alongside blogs by fans, coaches, cheerleaders, and managers, there are plenty by professional sports journalists, many of whom have found blogging a good way to interact with fans – who always relish the opportunity to lambast or support an opinion.

13 Blogging & politics

Political bloggers have played a significant role in catapulting blogs into the mainstream media spotlight. After the events of 9/11 and the subsequent attention that blogging received, many professional and amateur pundits signed up to voice their views on the policies of the United States and her allies.

Warblogging

As we've seen (see p.12), **warblogs** were the most attention-grabbing of the early political blogs. The first to strike were conservative bloggers, channeling their obsession with what they saw as a biased liberal media into sites promoting the White House's pro-war agenda. In response, anti-war bloggers entered the blogosphere in large numbers. Soon there was an intensely cross-linked environment that served to inform, educate, and infuriate the public.

Blogging has also been a source of expression for people living in current or potential combat zones. Blogs from the volatile Middle East have found an audience among readers for their first-hand perspectives and information unavailable through regular media channels. Salam Pax was the first to make a major impact (see p.12), but since then many bloggers from Iraq, Afghanistan, China, Korea, and Iran have adopted blogs as a means to share their stories with an international audience. For example:

We Are Iran: The Persian Blogs

Author Nasrin Alavi's 2006 Soft Skull Press publication highlights the best representations of the Persian blogosphere's struggle for free expression.

The Korean Blog List korea.banoffeepie.com

An English-language blog portal on Korea composed by Koreans (with the occasional entry by a non-Korean).

War zones have also given birth to a subset of weblogs known as **Milblogs**, which focus on the war from the perspective of active or retired military personnel.

Mudville Gazette www.mudvillegazette.com

Site penned by a soldier serving in Germany. Filled with views, news, and lots of links to other Milblogs.

Smash www.indepundit.com
Citizen Smash fought in one incarnation of America's war on terror, and has since returned to civilian life. His site links to an extensive list of other Milblogs.

Blackfive www.blackfive.net/main/2005/05/milblogs.html
An extensive list of Milblogs broken into categories like Army in Iraq, Spouse, Family & Friends, and Bloggers killed in action.

Hoder

Hossein Derakhshan, the Johnny Appleseed of Persian bloggers who now lives safely in Toronto, combined his technical knowhow with blogger services to create a free tool enabling **Persian characters** on blogspot pages. Derakhshan's site, written in both Farsi and English, focuses mainly on Iranian politics.

English www.hoder.com/weblog
Farsi www.i.hoder.com

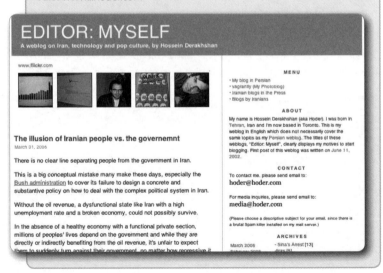

Right versus left

Most political blogs have an openly defined liberal or conservative bias. Impartiality is hardly a concern for most political bloggers, and they are unafraid to let their political leanings influence their writing. Major news sources have to enrobe themselves with at least the appearance of impartiality, but bloggers are free to say what they want, how they want.

Because political blogs are generally maintained by individuals, political stances are unlikely to fit perfectly within pre-determined party lines. A so-called conservative blogger might support the Bush administration's push to drill for oil in the **Alaskan Wildlife Refuge**, say, but be against his frothing religious moralism and hand-holding of Saudi princes. As such, bloggers from across the political divide may find the opportunity to unite on certain issues.

Free Republic www.freerepublic.com

Though not technically a blog, Free Republic has had a major influence on the political blogosphere. James Robinson, a political commentator, started to use bulletin boards to voice his politics in the early 1990s. In 1996, he launched Free Republic as a forum for discussion of conservative politics, and as an activist site for grassroots conservatism. It became a hangout for Clinton-bashers during the impeachment controversy, and contributed heavily to the Rathergate affair (see p.13).

The Drudge Report www.drudgereport.com

This popular news site run by Matt Drudge started in 1994 as a weekly subscriber-based email. It went online shortly after and became known for its incessant coverage of the news, gossip, and rumors surrounding President Clinton. The site was the first news source to break the Monica Lewinsky scandal, eventually leading to the re-election slogan "Rather blow jobs, than no jobs." As the sole proprietor of the Drudge Report, Matt Drudge was unafraid to bring his biases to the forefront and used his website to file stories that were often characterized as careless, reckless, and malicious. The current format of the Drudge Report resembles an out-of-control blog (with entries and links thrown together onto one chaotic page), but is not called a blog by its author.

The 2004 US election

By 2004, political bloggers had already contributed to the ousting of Senator Trent Lott (see p.13) and were being taken seriously by both politicians and the established news network. During that year's presidential election, bloggers were swarming around information, making connections, fact checking, and presenting their results to the public at large. For the first time, political bloggers were recognized by the Republican and Democratic parties as viable news sources, and were invited to conventions as card-carrying members of the press.

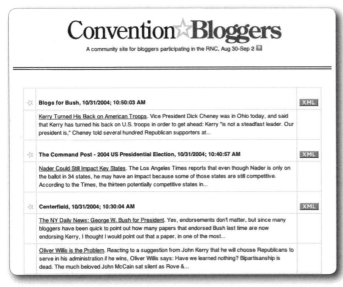

Presidential hopefuls Howard Dean and Wesley Clark gained popularity on the Internet among bloggers before they were taken seriously by traditional media outlets. And Howard Dean's **Blog for America** blog (see p.15) helped to raise a record amount of money for his nomination campaign. Pushed along by a strong Internet presence, both Dean and Clark were at one point considered front-runners for the Democratic nomination before eventually losing to John Kerry. When the campaign was down to the last two, both Kerry and Bush took a page from the also-rans and started blogging the road to the election.

Creating influence

Compared to the mass media, the vast majority of blogs have tiny readerships, and yet political bloggers as a whole manage to exert a tremendous amount of influence. Partly this is because hot leads and breaking news reported by small blogs can quickly spread through the entire Web if picked up by an A-list blogger. In this sense, an elite blog like **Instapundit** or **AndrewSullivan** serves as an information aggregator, so media and opinion leaders need only read one or two blogs before getting a good idea of what the entire blogosphere is buzzing about.

As blogs, and bloggers, gain credibility with the media, they have appeared as pundits on various news programs, been asked to write op-ed pieces, and many opinion journals. *The New Republic*, *The Spectator*, the *Washington Monthly*, *New Criterion*, *Salon*, and the *National Review* now sponsor individual bloggers or have developed their own blogs. The websites of Fox News, ABC News and MSNBC all host their own blogs, and it is now de rigueur for the mainstream to quote from and credit blogs.

National Review
corner.nationalreview.com
The New Republic
www.tnr.com/blog/theplank
New Criterion www.newcriterion.com/weblog/armavirumque.html
Salon www.salon.com/blogs
The Spectator
www.spectator.co.uk/blog
Washington Monthly
www.washingtonmonthly.com

Blogging a revolution

Blogs have been especially useful for communicating in repressive societies. Where the media is under direct government supervision, speaking against the rule of law is often punishable by methods considered cruel or inhumane by critics in the West. With carefully maintained anonymity, bloggers in these parts of the world can send a global message once only transferable by smudged underground newspapers and grainy-typed pamphlets.

In Iran, most of the reformist papers have been shut down, leaving a void where journalists and writers would otherwise express themselves. Into that breech stepped revolutionaries armed with blogs. Blogs became a popular, unregulated source of news and commentary, and many younger Iranians flocked to them for disseminating and absorbing information.

While it took some time for the Iranian government to catch onto the subversive power of blogs, once they found out, t hey were swift to act. Beginning as early as 2003, bloggers in Iran were arrested, interrogated, and even jailed for charges ranging from morality violations to insulting political leaders. By 2005, the Iranian government was systematically blocking political websites and blogs in an aggressive attempt at crushing connections between any potentially dissident factions.

Blogs that are used to criticize governments are nothing new, but a political environment such as Iran's is difficult to tread. Despite this, blogging remains a key form of communication for Iranians, and it is estimated that there are more than 100,000 active bloggers in "**weblogistan**." The overall number of Persian bloggers has pushed Farsi (the 28th most spoken language in the world) to the fourth most used language in the blogosphere. Maintaining a blog is now common, not just for censored journalists and teenagers, but for student organizers, ex-pats, and even Muslim clerics.

Iranian blogger Bijan Safsari writes on bijan-safsari.com, "At a time when our society is deprived of its rightful free means of communication, and our newspapers are being closed down one by one – with writers and journalists crowding the corners of our jails, the only realm that can safeguard and shoulder the responsibility of free speech is the blogosphere."

Freedom of expression

In 2005, Reporters Without Borders, an international organization interested in issues relating to freedom of speech, released an online book entitled *Handbook For Bloggers And Cyber-Dissidents*. Aside from offering tutorials on how to set up and maintain blogs, this book gives advice on how to use blogs as a voice of dissent – including tips on how to avoid trouble within repressive governments. The theme of the book is freedom of expression, and it highlights the role that blogs can play in constructing an independent media resource.

In China, where the government uses an Internet filtering system to block "disruptive" websites, numerous blogs have been shut down for real or imagined infractions. In 2005, a law mandated that all non-profit website owners must register their sties with their real personal information, a development that drastically heightened the personal risks of blogging against the government.

And it's not just the offending government taking part in these repressive acts. American software giant **Microsoft** has admitted to partnering with Chinese authorities to censor the Internet. Politically sensitive words like freedom, democracy, and human rights are automatically removed from Microsoft's newly launched Chinese blogging software. Microsoft insists that these restrictions were the price the company had to pay to spread the positive benefits of blogs (while downplaying their strategic positioning for billions of Chinese Yuan).

Chinese bloggers have found it increasingly difficult to make their voices heard, and in response to their plight, the blogosphere has offered up "Adopt a Chinese Blog". Bloggers using independent hosting services have been asked to host blocked blogs from China, thus providing a wormhole through the government's censoring software. This method disperses the otherwise illegal blogs across many servers internationally, meaning there is no effective way for the Chinese government to track and shut down every single blog. The blogosphere coming together in this fashion is a powerful testament to the strength of the blogging community.

Adopt a Blog www.adoptablog.org

Blogging & journalism

Blogs have indisputably enhanced the way information travels (and sticks) in our media grid. But the relationship between blogs and the traditional media hasn't always been cosy. For a while, professional news hounds decried amateur journalists' credibility, dismissing bloggers as unsubstantiated and unimportant voices; bloggers struck back by exposing the lack of integrity in professional media organizations. These days, there's less antipathy between the two groups, and also less of a clear distinction: the journalistic value of the blogosphere is more widely recognized, and many mainstream media outlets have their own blogs.

Blogs as media watchdogs

Professional journalists now have an independent, amorphous entity scrutinizing their output. Bloggers have proven adept at picking up discarded or lightly covered stories, and then aggressively fact-checking and pursuing them until traditional media sources are forced to renew their attention.

As we've seen (see p.13), this type of scrutiny has enabled bloggers to claim the heads of public figures such as Senator Trent Lott, CNN's chief news executive, Eason Jordan; and editor of the *New York Times*, Howell Raines. In each case, bloggers honed in on stories or statements that would have otherwise slipped through the cracks, fanning the flames until the issues were resolved.

Eason Jordan www.easongate.com

On February 2005, Eason Jordan resigned as CNN's chief news executive amidst controversy over his remarks made during an off-the-record panel discussion at the **World Economic Forum** in Switzerland. Eason suggested that the US military had targeted journalists in war zones, a comment that only came to light after a forum attendee posted an online account. The mainstream media were initially slow to pick up on the controversy, but were eventually forced to cover the story after right-wing bloggers brought the statement to national attention.

EASONGATE.COM

Jeff Gannon

Liberal bloggers forced the resignation of James Guckert, White House correspondent of conservative news site **Talon News**. It was revealed that Guckert wasn't a journalist at all and had been simultaneously writing under a false name for a Republican activist group. Bloggers even found nude pictures of Guckert online, which he had posted in an effort to solicit sex for money. Even after resigning from Talon News, Guckert has continued to use the name Gannon and is now a columnist for a gay and lesbian website.

Presenting alternative viewpoints

Blogs enable the broadcasting of non-mainstream viewpoints. People who want to bypass mainstream media can do so using all manner of written words, images, live audio, and video to fill out their versions of an event.

Backfence www.backfence.com

Grassroots journalism takes on a whole new meaning when anyone can become a reporter. Mark Potts, a onetime reporter for the *Washington Post* and co-founder of washingtonpost.com, started Backfence in 2004 hoping to spread the practice of **open-source journalism**. Backfence. com is focused on "hyper-local" community news generated by the public. Under-the-radar news on school plays and local soccer league scores are the focus of Backfence. So far, Backfence has only been employed in three suburban locales near Washington, DC. Potts hopes to expand to major metropolitan areas in the near future.

Dateline Earth blog.seattlepi.nwsource.com/environment

Seattle Post-Intelligencer reporters serve up local environmental happenings and tidbits from around the globe.

Bush Greenwatch www.bushgreenwatch.org

Tracking the Bush administration's environmental misdeeds.

BushGreenwatch { TRACKING THE BUSH ADMINISTRATION'S ENVIRONMENTAL MISDEEDS. }

Jerry Brown jerrybrown.org/blog

Former Governor of California and current Mayor of Oakland uses his blog to bypass the mainstream media and communicate directly with his constituents – much to the chagrin of Jello Biafra.

Blogs from the pros

Weblogs can be used to report or discuss issues that fall outside the scope of print publications – bloggers are free to explore issues in as much detail as they want. As such, even professional journalists have found the format refreshing. Blogs are being used by major media outlets as a supplement to their more traditional output, giving reporters room to expand on a topic in a more casual tone.

Andrew Sullivan www.andrewsullivan.com

A former columnist and editor at *The New Republic*, Andrew Sullivan also hosts one of the most popular blogs on the Web. The site captures the somewhat paradoxical personal-political views of this HIV-positive, practicing Roman Catholic gay conservative. Sullivan is an advocate of blog journalism and became one of the first mainstream journalists to experiment with blogging when in 2000 he launched the Daily Dish (now hosted by time.blogs.com).

PressThink www.pressthink.org

Jay Rosen teaches Journalism at **New York University** and has served as Chair of the Department since 1999. His blog focuses on topics such as citizen journalism and the ordeals that journalists face working within the current media system. PressThink won the Reporters Without Borders award for outstanding defense of free expression in 2005.

RConversation rconversation.blogs.com

TV-reporter-turned-blogger Rebecca MacKinnon writes and speaks on the future of media in the Internet age, freedom of speech online, and the Internet in China. She is a co-founder of Global Voices Online (see p.22) and a current Research Fellow at Harvard Law School's Berkman Center for Internet & Society. MacKinnon's research and interests focus on blogs and participatory media, especially as they relate to enhancing the capabilities of journalism.

First-person reporting

During the 9/11 attack, the tsunami in Asia, and the hurricanes in the United States, bloggers were able to report from a position on the very inside – from places unreachable by the traditional media. You can explore some of these first-person reports via the following links.

First-person coverage of the tsunami (via Boing Boing)
www.boingboing.net/2004/12/27/bloggers_in_se_asia_.html
List of Hurricane Katrina bloggers
www.artsjournal.com/aboutlastnight/archives20050828.shtml#102347

15 Educational blogging

It didn't take long for teachers to embrace blogging's powerful organizational capabilities and ease of use. Educators from elementary to graduate school are finding ways to turn blogs into learning aids, using them to create projects, offer feedback, post assignments, and evaluate class progress. And students are encouraged to use blogs to create virtual communities and to reflect on classroom discussions.

Weblogg-ed www.weblogg-ed.com
Will Richardson, teacher and author of a book on using Web tools in classrooms, maintains this blog that touches on all issues regarding the use of blogging (and **Podcasting**) in education.

Adventures in Educational Blogging ssedro.blogspot.com
A fifth-grade teacher from Minnesota documents her experiences trying to incorporate social technologies (i.e. blogs) into her curriculum.

My Name is Meredith weblogs.hcrhs.k12.nj.us/meredithf
Meredith used her classroom blog to pull together resources for researching Africa. Not only does she report on the news she finds, she also tries to practice her writing and interviewing with stories she creates herself. The blog has sections displaying her homework and a log of her overall

progress. It's no longer updated, but still a good example of blogging's educational power.

AP Calculus Peer Help calhelp.blogspot.com

Started by a student (Sarah) hoping to help other students on their way to taking the AP Calculus test, this site is "a place where we can all talk about what we don't understand, what we need a little more work on, or what needs to be explained a little more."

Ellie's Math Blog grade7math.blogspot.com

An online space for Ellie and other seventh graders to get help and learn math. Ellie's blog features links to Problems of the Week, a Middle School Math Dictionary, and other Grade Seven math blogs.

Building educational communities

Blogs are being used to draw students together into scholastic communities. Educators know that students write better, and more often, when they have an audience – by setting up a classroom site where students can create and maintain individual blogs, they create a **mini-blogosphere** that enhances the real-world learning environment. Students are encouraged to post additional commentary on assigned readings and classroom discussions, and to bring up topics of individual interest.

The Georgia-NJ Connection weblogs.hcrhs.k12.nj.us/georgia

Two writing classes, one in Georgia and one in New Jersey, work together to become better journalists. Students are given the task of researching and then reporting their findings. Through their blogs, they can also comment and cross-link with each other, fostering discussion and conversation.

educational blogging

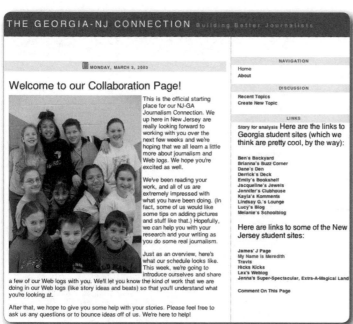

The site features the individual blogs of the students, as well as collaborative reports and stories.

Assigned Reading Blog

weblogs.hcrhs.k12.nj.us/beesbook

Students at Hunterdon Central Regional High School in New Jersey collaborated to produce this group blog about their book-reading assignment, *The Secret Life of Bees*. Students took turns discussing the themes and symbols, and posted general analyses of the book. The blog also incorporates student-created artworks inspired by the story.

Elementary schools

While student blogs have proven to be useful for middle- and high-school students, younger, elementary-school children are just being introduced to blogging. Kids as young as first-graders get involved by creating drawings and writings that are then scanned and uploaded to a blog for parents to see at home.

Studio Four-News

www.columbia.k12.mo.us/she/mvillasa/S4news .htm

Fourth-graders at Shepard Elementary School in Columbia, Missouri are assigned to be class reporters for a day. These young news hounds are responsible for recording the day's events on the class blog and incorporating action photos where appropriate.

Hangleton Junior School (Hove, Sussex) www.hangletonweblogs.org

One school in the United Kingdom has students as young as seven years of age using weblogs as part of their normal academic routine. After setting up a popular **after-school club** about blogging, teachers found that the children were reading at literacy levels far above their age group. The students also used blogs as a dynamic way to improve their computer skills – learning to copy and paste, change fonts, and create short blog entries.

Teachers blog too

It's not only students that maintain blogs. Many teachers use blogging to share curriculums, discuss educational methods that would benefit their students, or to give the wider public an insight into their world. Blogs have even been used in tandem, where a veteran teacher mentors an entry-year teacher, and both blog about the experience.

TLN Teacher Voices

tln.typepad.com/tln_voices

This site boils down listserv discussions between 300 accomplished teachers across the United States and Canada.

Brighton's Hope

www.teacherleaders .org/BRblog.html

Former National Teacher of the Year (2003) Betsy Rogers chronicles her work in one of Alabama's highest-need elementary schools. Her touching stories expose the day-to-day struggle of Brighton's efforts to transform itself into a high-achieving school.

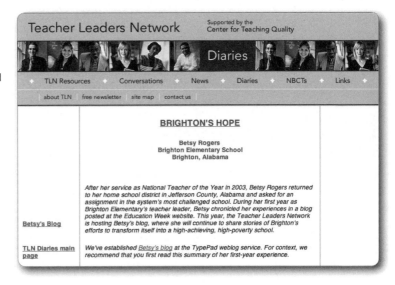

educational blogging

MB Matthews: Street Smarts
From the Frontlines of Urban Education

Street Smarts mbmatthews.blogspot.com
Mary Beth Matthews shares her frustrations as a teacher working in an under-funded inner-city school. Her blog keeps the community up-to-date on school events and discusses how political policy affects their school system. Says Matthews, "I am publishing this journal in response to those who are quick to criticize 'those lazy, greedy, teachers.' I offer you a glimpse into my world."

First Year Teacher Diary firstyearteacher.blogspot.com
An anonymous first-year teacher in Rocky Mount, North Carolina documents her experiences working for the Teach for America campaign.

NWA Voices ccmug.blogspot.com
Students in John Blake's classroom at North Whiteville Academy use Podcasts to study science concepts and in the process strengthen their computer skills. Blake uses the blog to post reflections on his method and thoughts on how to better incorporate shared media into the classroom.

Parents and the community

Parents and school administrators aren't leaving themselves out of the educational blog equation, either. A **classroom blog** keeps parents in touch with due dates, daily assignments, and upcoming tests and quizzes, while general school blogs point to upcoming events.

Knowing Henry knowinghenry.blogspot.com
This blog's author, Kevin Peter, is an active parent of C.W. Henry School in Philadelphia. Peter and his wife host monthly meetings where they introduce current Henry parents to each other, and use their blog to share real-world experience of life inside the public school.

Flushing International High School www.flushinginternational.org
This secondary school uses its blog to update staff, students, and parents about school news and upcoming events. The principal of FIHS also maintains a blog that features helpful ideas for quickly improving immigrant students' English skills.

Meriwether Lewis Elementary School www.lewiselementary.org
Lewis Elementary's blog highlights upcoming school activities, classroom updates, principal's notes, inclement weather reports, and recent school news.

Books, Books, Books librarygoddess.blogspot.com
A high-school librarian reviews books written for teens.

Blogging in college

Higher-education blogs are being used for many of the same reasons they're being used in grade schools. With the ease of publishing that blogging offers, professors can quickly update their class blogs and provide an **information base** for students. Class materials such as notes and assignments become part of the site, and students from across the country (and world) form connections over high-level debates.

Purdue University Business Writing Blog
joe.english .purdue.edu/fa05/420S1
This blog for business-writing students at Purdue University was set up as the default meeting place for the class. The site is used to collaborate on writing projects, lists pathways to blogs written by students of the course, and holds a class calendar, completed projects, and ongoing debates over course content.

Professors and students speak up

Blogs can take discussions from the classroom – where time constraints often lead to shortened sound bites – onto the infinite land mass of the Internet. A heated debate between two students might be a waste of classroom time, but on a course blog it makes

educational blogging

Why even attend class?

Much to the delight of slackers everywhere, an instructor at Johns Hopkins is offering his lectures on his course's blog as a **Podcast**. With the ease of recording and publishing that Podcasting offers, more professors are likely to use it as an alternative or supplement to posting class notes. Now you really can lie in bed and go to class at the same time.

for exciting and stimulating reading. And professors that receive emails from students can post their responses for everyone to see, saving them the trouble of answering the same question repeatedly. Courses that upkeep a blog from year to year can become a treasure trove of information.

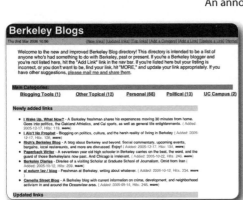

Biz Deans Talk www.deanstalk.net
Deans from top business schools in America and Europe gather on this blog to discuss Management Education.

Research Blogs huminf.uib.no/~jill/txt/researchblogs.html
An annotated list of blogs used by researchers and academics. The annotations explain what kind of research each blogger does and how each weblog is used in their endeavors.

Edtec Student's Daily johns_edtec_blog.blogspot.com
John chronicles his journey through the Educational Technology graduate program at San Diego State University.

Berkeley Blogs www.berkeleyblogs.org
The University of California at Berkeley has led the charge for scholastic blogging since day one. Their blog directory contains personal blogs from students, administrators, and alumni; and the popular **CalStuff** blog keeps the campus informed of upcoming academic and social events.

Colgate Conversations

www.colgate.edu/DesktopDefault1.aspx?tabid=2389&pgID=6018

Colgate Conversations are Podcasts that feature faculty members, alumni, administrators, and students talking about cutting-edge research projects, higher-education issues, careers after college, and life on campus.

16 Blogging & business

Companies of all shapes and sizes are starting to experiment with blogging – for communicating with customers, for advertising and marketing purposes, for improving customer service, and for making themselves seem more "human." Starting a blog helps companies be a part of a conversation, opening up their ears to valuable feedback (including stinging criticism) from the public.

Communicating with customers

Instead of sending out emails, many businesses have embraced blogs as an effective means of reaching out to customers and clients. Links to official press releases, product reviews, and industry or company-related news – all become fodder for the company blog. A couple of examples:

Primal Records www.primalrecords.com
Primal Records, a record store located in Berkeley, California, uses its blog

to keep customers abreast of new releases, company news, special offers, in-store events, and inventory updates. The site allows customers to leave feedback on everything from store policies to news about local parties. This allows Primal to stay keyed in to what its customers want.

GM's Fastlane fastlane.gmblogs.com General Motors has a thriving blog manned primarily by VP of Communications for North America, Gary Grates, but also including con- tributions form other **GM staffers** (such as the occasional post from Vice Chairman and auto-industry legend Bob Lutz). The hundreds of comments posted to Fastlane are all reviewed before being uploaded, but very few are deleted. Grates loves the

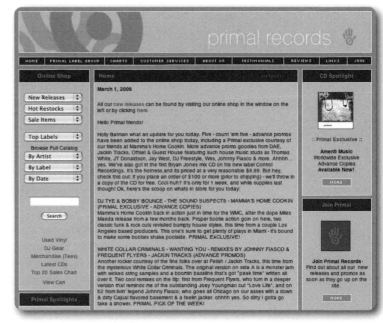

Fortune 500 Business Blogging Wiki

In an attempt to provide some answers to the question "Are blogs good for business?", Chris Anderson of *Wired* magazine and Ross Mayfield of **Socialtext**, a social software provider, has compiled a list of Fortune 500 Companies and is tracking which ones choose to blog. Businees Blogs have been defined by them as "Active public blogs by company employees about the company and/or its products." Their endeavor is in its early stages and the blogs haven't been thoroughly indexed or categorized, but what they hope to do is create a Business Blogging Index that will compare the stock performance of compa- nies that blog with those that don't. For more information, see www. socialtext.net/bizblogs

comments made by passionate customers and says the blog serves as a valuable source of constructive feedback.

Marketing & advertising

Blogs can be an excellent way of providing targeted advertising. There exist blogs that discuss, and review, every category of product under the sun. Many of these sites build a loyal following and a review on these blogs can influence thousands of readers. By submitting products for independent review, companies can receive feedback on their product and reach a targeted audience all at once.

Even without hawking products or services, many blogs count on advertising as their revenue stream. A topic-specific blog already draws a targeted audience and advertisers can take advantage of that narrow focus by buying space on the blog or website. Small businesses also benefit tremendously as the cost required to advertise on a blog is minuscule compared to the budgets required for print and television placement.

Furthermore, once a blogger links to a review, or to a company's website, that one link can multiply and shoot the article or site to

the top of a search engine or **blog topic aggregator**. A hot item can traverse the blogosphere incredibly quickly, powering amazing results and attracting worldwide attention.

Project Blog www.projectblog.com
Richards Interactive specializes in helping clients create online content for marketing purposes (they handled the Nokia 3650 campaign; see box). The company finds bloggers with loyal followings who are willing to try products from matching companies. The company does not pay bloggers or provide direct

The Nokia blog

Mobile phone giant Nokia used bloggers to help launch a new phone in 2003. Nokia gave a handful of bloggers their new **3650 camera phone** in the hope that they would like the product and blog about it. The bloggers were under no obligation to mention the phone or Nokia but the majority of them did within a few months of using the product. The positive testimonials that resulted from this effort to incorporate blogs into an overall marketing strategy demonstrated that low-cost blogs can deliver.

compensation, except for allowing them to keep the devices. The products are reviewed based on their own merits and Richards Interactive has no control over the type of feedback resulting from the testing.

Building buzz

Many promotional blogs are set up in advance of product launches, offering teaser items such as exclusive downloads, screenshots, demos, interviews, and breaking news. Buzz sites containing behind-the-scenes journals have also become a popular way for authors, musicians, and filmmakers to build hype for their upcoming releases.

Adaptation www.susanorlean.com/adaptation

Before the release of the movie *Adaptation*, a publicity blog was set up on author Susan Orlean's website (whose novel *The Orchid Thief* was the subject of the translation). Penned by unaffiliated blogger **Jason Kottke**, the blog was an obsessively updated news site covering the production process and linking to trailers, reviews, and interviews with the cast and director. The blog eventually shut down after the release of the *Adaptation* DVD, but on the whole this early attempt at incorporating blogs into marketing plans worked very well.

Dr Pepper and Raging Cow

In March 2003, Dr Pepper/Seven Up Inc. attempted to build buzz for a new flavored milk product, Raging Cow, by hiring bloggers to mention and endorse the product on their sites. After it was revealed that the company had explicitly asked not to be revealed as paying the bloggers to peddle a product, the blogosphere reacted vehemently. Citing **corruption of integrity**, bloggers called for a boycott. Professional media outlets were called upon to disclose their promotional ties, and bloggers felt that this standard should be applied to the amateur blogging world.

Despite a poor reception by some of the blogosphere, the campaign was marked a success by the company. Reaction to the humorous Raging Cow blog (penned from the perspective of the cow at raging-cowblog.clickhere.com) was positive, especially from the target audience of teenagers. The blog campaign was intended to raise grassroot awareness and this mission was accomplished. The Raging Cow story marked one of the first times that a mainstream company used blogs for marketing purposes – even if it also touched off a firestorm of blogosphere controversy.

Pasteurize This!

Customer service

Many businesses use blogs as a supplement to traditional customer support services. When things go wrong, customers want immediate solutions – a blog can help allay consumer anxiety by explaining service shutdowns and providing updates and fixes. Unlike over-busy customer service phonelines, easily accessible customer service blogs distribute answers quickly and efficiently, cutting down on stress for customers and employees alike.

Macromedia www.macromedia.com/community
One of the first companies to adopt blogs for customer service was software maker Macromedia, which used bloggers after the launch of new

product versions back in 2002. Five employees were designated "community managers" and tasked with answering users' questions while showing developers how to take full advantage of the revised software's newest features. The blogs quickly grew into fully fledged online communities where developers would share their experiences using the programs – and Macromedia absorbed plenty of user feedback. While the blogosphere was initially resistant to Macromedia's perceived efforts at commercializing blogs, that stance soon softened and bloggers eventually lauded the company for being on the cutting edge of blogging.

Blogger Status status.blogger.com

Blogger (see p.36) provides excellent customer support for both paid and unpaid users via its meticulously updated Blogger Status blog. The blog keeps users informed about continued development, upgrades, and service outages. When server problems, bugs, or errors are sweeping across the platform, Blogger tells users what's happening, and what's being done to resolve the situation.

Product enhancement

Other companies are using blogs to give their customers a sense of added value for their purchase. A software developer might blog a nifty feature that would otherwise be overlooked by the casual user, while a publisher might establish an author's blog to keep the public informed of a book's latest developments.

Fast Company blog.fastcompany.com

Fast Company, a magazine dedicated to cutting-edge entrepreneurs, uses their blog to enhance their print publication. Employees blog about any topic that interests them, presuming their interests intersect with those of their readers. The blog discusses business ideas with readers and allows the magazine to promote its own products and maintain an ongoing informal interaction with their customers.

Coudal www.coudal.com

Coudal Partners, an advertising and design firm based out of Chicago, maintains a blog that exhibits their current projects, links to articles about advertising history, outside projects of general interest, and basically anything else they think is cool. The idea is to showcase the agency's creations next to the best external examples of advertising design. No longer simply a promotional tool, Coudal's blog has become a respected resource for design aficionados everywhere.

Customer Evangelists Blog

customerevangelists.typepad .com/blog

Based upon their research into grassroots marketing campaigns and the power of Internet communities, Ben McConnell and Jackie Huba have co-written a book entitled *Creating Customer Evangelists*. They suggest that including consumers in the everyday operations of an organization gives them a sense of input that's otherwise nonexistent. As a result of this connection, ordinary customers can become product "evangelists," and thereby be born again as unpaid promoters.

Providing expertise

Blogging can be a great way to impart expert knowledge, which in turn can be a great way to promote professional services. As with any vendor or agent, with increased credibility and higher visibility come more clients. Two good examples are blogs by lawyers – commonly referred to as **blawgs** – and real-estate agents.

Law blogs

Dennis Kennedy www.denniskennedy.com/blog

As a technology and intellectual property lawyer who is also a tech expert, Kennedy uses his blog (and website) as promotion for his consulting

and speaking services. Samples of his writing and seminar offerings are available, as well as a comprehensive list of free legal resources. Kennedy has won the TechnoLawyer Syndicated Contributor of the Year award so many times that it has been renamed in his honor.

The Trademark Blog www.schwimmerlegal.com

The prototypical example of how to use engaging writing and eye-catching pictures to create a compelling practice-specific blog. Maintained by Schwimmer Mitchell Law Firm, based out of Westchester, New York, the blog focuses on **trademark**, **copyright**, and **domain name law**, and offers advice and analysis to lay people.

Groklaw www.groklaw.net

Pamela Jones started Groklaw as a way to meld her legal experience with her journalistic training. The result is a legal research resource for lawyers and non-lawyers alike. Her initial idea was to follow one intellectual property case daily, explaining what was happening in common terms as the case moved through the courts. Eventually Groklaw attracted more contributors and expanded to cover patent and standards law as well.

Declan McCullagh's Politech www.politechbot.com

In the oldest Internet resource devoted to politics and technology, journalist and programmer Declan McCullagh surveys the fertile terrain where law, culture, technology, and politics meet.

Realty blogs

Matrix matrix.millersamuel.com

Jonathan Miller, president of several real-estate appraisal firms, pens this blog to share his analysis and advice on the real-estate market and is the author of a series of online real-estate market reports. Miller's stand-out blog empowers consumers, helping them make better choices and obtain services at better prices.

Toronto at Home toreal.blogs.com

A beautifully organized real-estate blog focusing on market trends in the Toronto area. Daily updates discuss issues like mortgage rates and financial forecasting, developing homes in hot new areas, and how to interpret a realtor's lingo.

Curbed www.curbed.com

The center of the virtual conversation about real estate in New York (with a separate website for Los Angeles), Curbed also provides frequent updates about trends and the market in general. Curbed holds the honor of being the most-trafficked real-estate site on the Web.

Start-ups

Blogs targeted at helping the small business owner have increasingly gained popularity in the blogosphere. Whether the blogs focus on writing a business plan, managing workers or finding the most effective telemarketing methods, readers have found that blogs are excellent resources.

Duct Tape Marketing www.ducttapemarketing.com/weblog.php

John Jantsch is a marketing coach, consultant, speaker, writer, and author who uses his blog as a hub for his small business marketing products. Jantsch establishes credibility with potential customers by blogging about useful marketing techniques combined with analysis of **emerging trends**.

Fresh Inc blog.inc.com

Inc.com writers share their thoughts on current events, business issues, and news. They specialize in providing resources, ideas, and advice for entrepreneurs and home-based businesses.

Business Blogs www.allbusiness.com/blog/metablog.asp
A collection of small business blogs from around the Web.

Small Business Pod www.smallbizpod.co.uk
A UK Podcast designed to help "news, interviews, and practical advice for small and medium-sized businesses, start-ups and entrepreneurs."

Adding personality to the mix

Besides pushing products and providing customer support, blogs are being used by businesses to build rapport with consumers. To this aim, many companies are encouraging individual employees to blog, and aren't limiting them to company- or industry-specific topics. Microsoft's Scobleizer (see p.16) is one such example. Others include:

Google Blogs googleblog.blogspot.com
Aside from its blog about upcoming services, Google employees are encouraged to blog openly and to blog often. Company jargon is explained, anecdotes are shared, and online visitors are given an inside view into the Googleplex's unique business culture.

Signs Never Sleep signsneversleep.typepad.com
The owner of a New England-based wooden sign shop, the **Lincoln Sign Company**, blogs the process of creating hand-made signage for customers. During his posts, he not only discusses the history and craftsmanship involved in his work, but also his day-to-day experiences with customers. His blog helps potential customers get to know him and trust his work, as well as advertising his full range of products.

Blogging from the top

It's not just regular employees who are blogging. It adds sincerity to the corporate message when a high-ranking executive addresses and interacts with the public in an open forum. **CEOs** and other top-floor employees have found that blogs let them respond to media and industry critiques while simultaneously discussing the finer points of their golf swing.

Sun Microsystems blogs.sun.com/jonathan

President and CEO of server maker Sun Microsystems, Jonathan Schwartz started a blog in 2004 and has consistently maintained it since. He mostly posts about his company and their rivals, but occasionally drops in tidbits on his personal life and travels. Over 1,000 other Sun employees maintain blogs, and Schwartz has lauded these bloggers for helping maintain Sun's reputation as an authentic tech company: "Everyone blogging at Sun is verifying that we possess a culture of tenacity and authenticity."

Edelman Worldwide www.edelman.com/speak_up/blog

CEO Richard Edelman of Edelman Worldwide (the world's largest public relations firm) maintains a pundit-style blog that highlights trends and issues in communications and media. Edelman is a big proponent of blogs as business tools.

Blog Maverick www.blogmaverick.com

Mark Cuban, owner of the NBA **Dallas Mavericks**, blogs on marketing schemes, free agency, the current state of refereeing, and sometimes just as a fan of the game. Cuban is also an active investor in cutting-edge technologies and will sometimes include his take on these matters, too. His colloquial tone is reflective of many of the best exec blogs: a blog that reflects the personality of its writer is always engaging and, when that

writer happens to be a billionaire at the helm of a major company, it can make for gripping reading.

In-house blogging

While blogs are usually available to everyone with an Internet connection, many companies are starting to make use of private blogs accessible by employees only. In these contexts, blogs can act as virtual hubs for organizing documents and coordinating projects.

So-called **K-blogs** (knowledge blogs) are designed primarily to aid organization, housing meeting minutes and spreading information quickly among employees. In bigger companies where information tends to disseminate slowly, blogs help tremendously by providing a central "brain dump" with automatic archive and search tools.

Project blogs, meanwhile, aim to allow teams to work more effectively on a group task. They list deadlines and serve as a repository for notes and ideas. One employee might be sent off to a convention, say, tasked with taking notes, which can then be shared with the rest of the team via the blog. This avoids information getting lost between various inboxes and multiple versions of attached documents.

The
blogroll

Blogroll contents

Art blogs	161	Metro blogs	173
Blogs about blogs	163	Miscellaneous interests	174
Blog awards	163	Oddities	175
Business blogs	163	Personal	176
Car blogs	164	Pets	178
Celebrity blogs	165	Photoblogs	178
Design blogs	166	Political blogs	180
Food blogs	167	Pundit blogs	183
Gay & lesbian blogs	168	Sex blogs	185
Gossip blogs	168	Sports blogs	185
Insider blogs	169	Tech blogs	186
Knitting blogs	170	Personal tech blogs	188
Law blogs	170	Video blogs	189
Link blogs	171	Video games blogs	189
Literary blogs	172	Work/job blogs	190

The blogroll

Every good blog has a blogroll – a list of the author's favorite blogs – so why shouldn't a blogging book do the same? What follows is a selection of what we think are 250 (or so) of the blogosphere's most significant, interesting, or entertaining sites. Enjoy…

Art blogs (13)

Absolute Arts.com Blog blog.absolutearts.com
An assortment of artists, collectors, and dealers share their enthusiasm over Rembrandt exhibitions and Whiteread installations.

art.blogging.la (abLA) art.blogging.la
Part of the Metroblogging family, art.blogging.la is a Los Angeles-based art blog focusing on news, reviews, and upcoming events in the LA area.

Artopia www.artsjournal.com/artopia
Internationally oriented contemporary art criticism from long time industry insider, John Perreault.

Design Sponge designsponge.blogspot.com
Thoughts on contemporary design, with essays, articles, interviews, general musings and rants.

Drawn! drawn.ca
Collaborative Weblog for illustrators, artists, cartoonists, and anyone else who likes to draw.

Fecal Face www.fecalface.com
Supporting the SF and Bay Area art scene since 2000.

From the Floor fromthefloor.blogspot.com
Provocative entries from critic and lecturer Todd Gibson.

Gallery Hopper www.galleryhopper.org
A guide to the best of fine art photography, galleries, and events in New York City and beyond.

Modern Art Notes www.artsjournal.com/man
Thoughts and passions on contemporary and modern art from the well-respected Tyler Green.

My Paper Crane www.mypapercrane.com
Crafty projecs for the gentle artist inside us all.

We-Make-Money-Not-Art www.we-make-money-not-art.com
Nominated for Best European Blog 2006, this link blog unearths Internet treasures with alarming regularity.

Wish Jar Journal www.kerismith.com/blog
Keri Smith offers advice on how not to be so boring all the time.

Wooster Collective www.woostercollective.com
Dedicated to showcasing and celebrating ephemeral art placed on streets in cities around the world.

Blogs about blogs (2)

Blog Herald www.blogherald.com
Why critique reality when you can critique critiques of reality?

Bloglebrity www.blogebrity.com
Contains one version of the oft-quoted blogosphere A-, B-, and C-lists.

Blog awards (4)

Best of Blog (BoB) Awards www.thebestofblogs.com
Awards the best in personal blogs.

Bloggies www.bloggies.com
The most prominent blog awards features the best blogs in over thirty categories.

The BoBs: The Best of the Best International Competition www.thebobs.de
Deutsche Welle International Weblog Awards.

The Weblog Awards weblogawards.org
Each year this site compiles nearly a million votes in over twenty categories to find out who has the most popular blogs.

Business blogs (7)

Business Week's Blogspotting www.businessweek.com/the_thread/blogspotting
Where the worlds of business, media, and blogs collide.

Fast Company Now blog.fastcompany.com
Business magazine *Fast Company*'s Weblog is maintained by staffers, and features the occasional special guest or contributor.

Fresh Inc. blog.inc.com
With so much to say, the writers and editors of *Inc.* magazine just need a little more space to let loose.

Personal Development Blog www.stevepavlina.com/blog
Steve Pavlina, polyphasic sleeper, life coach and juggler, maintains this blog with a focus on "personal development for smart people."

ProBlogger www.problogger.net
Advises bloggers on earning money through smart advertising, well-formulated keywords, and carefully crafted content.

The Corporate Blogging Book blogwrite.blogs.com/book/
The author of *The Corporate Blogging Book* maintained this blog while writing her book.

The Long Tail www.thelongtail.com
Chris Anderson, editor-in-chief of *Wired* magazine, maintains a blog as he writes his book *The Long Tail*.

Car blogs (5)

Autoblog www.autoblog.com
Comes with everything but the sunroof.

Cars!Cars!Cars! carscarscars.blogs.com
An experienced auto writer analyses auto industry news and discusses real and impending problems with commenters.

Jalopnik www.jalopnik.com
Gawker's entry into the car enthusiast's world comes standard with frequent industry updates and features on concept cars and tricked-out rides.

Popular Mechanics Automotive Blog
www.popularmechanics.com/blog/automotive
The magazine's writers provide up-to-date news and information on the
auto industry.

The Truth About Cars www.thetruthaboutcars.com
Don't buy your new car until you read these two freelance automotive
journalists and their pal, the engineer.

Celebrity blogs (12)

Blog Maverick www.blogmaverick.com
Dallas Mavericks owner Mark Cuban brings his assertiveness to the blogosphere.

Dave Barry blogs.herald.com/dave_barrys_blog
Columnist, author, and Pulitzer prize-winning humorist Dave Barry offers
personal anecdotes alongside links to Barry Manilow calendars and inflat-
able penises.

David Byrne Journal journal.davidbyrne.com
Talking Heads frontman and post-punk innovator David Byrne blogs his
global movements and critiques the state of international politics.

Ian McKellen www.mckellen.com/cinema/lotr/journal.htm
Actor Ian McKellen kept a journal during the filming of *The Lord of the
Rings*; includes wizard beard maintenance tips (no current entries).

Jann Arden www.jannarden.com/journal.php
Canadian singer/songwriter Jann Arden's journal and fan pages.

Jason Mraz www.jasonmraz.com/journal
Singer/songwriter Jason Mraz writes lengthy blogs about life as a musician.

Margaret Cho www.margaretcho.net/blog
Comedienne and actress Margaret Cho uses her blog to post long entries on everything from politics and music to her new tattoo.

Neil Gaiman www.neilgaiman.com/journal
Creator of *Sandman* blogs the day-to-day process of writing, publishing, and promoting his current projects.

Princess Melissa www.princessmelissa.com
Real World contestant Melissa Howard blogs about triple Gs and celebreality.

The Naked Chef www.jamieoliver.com
British celebrity chef Jamie Oliver keeps his fans abreast of his cooking adventures.

William Gibson www.williamgibsonbooks.com/blog/blog.asp
A blog by the science fiction author and cyberpunk philosopher.

Zach Braff's Garden State Blog gardenstate.typepad.com
Braff started this blog to track his movie's release, now the *Scrubs* star uses it to keep his fans informed about upcoming works.

Design blogs (5)

Coudal Partners www.coudal.com
News, interviews, and links to the world of advertising and design. Very popular and beautifully designed.

Design Is Kinky www.designiskinky.net
Profiles cool and fresh young artists, and chronicles the creative process in the Insight section.

Design Observer www.designobserver.com
Presents intelligent discourse on issues surrounding design culture and business.

Stop Design www.stopdesign.com
Personal blog of graphic designer Douglas Bowman (responsible for redesigning the Blogger, Wired News, and Adaptive Path sites).

The Skinny blog.veer.com
The Weblog of design firm Veer, The Skinny is a repository of inspirational creations and insider information.

Food blogs (7)

A Hamburger Today www.ahamburgertoday.com
Looking for the world's best hamburger? So are the writers of this intensely focused food blog. They're also on the hunt for the best slice of pizza in New York (www.sliceny.com).

Chez Pim chezpim.typepad.com
Award-winning foodie blog based out of San Francisco.

David Lebovitz www.davidlebovitz.com
Acclaimed pastry chef David Lebovitz shares his stories, advice, and experiences.

Food Blog www.kiplog.com/food
Well-linked site showcasing recipes, ingredients, restaurants, and the best in food photography.

This Momma Cooks! mamarant.blogs.com/mamacooks
Motherly advice on cooking and cleaning; includes recipes, cookbook reviews, and product critiques.

What the Hell Does A Vegan Eat Anyway? veganmenu.blogspot.com
Vegans aren't so strange once you get to know them.

Well Fed Network www.wellfed.net
A collection of blogs serving up an online magazine, a trade journal, and a personal food diary.

Gay & lesbian blogs (3)

Boi From Troy boifromtroy.com
A glimpse in to the mind of a thirty-something gay Republican.

Gay Patriot www.gaypatriot.net
Where conservatism and homosexuality meet for brunch.

Gay Spirituality & Culture gayspirituality.typepad.com/blog
A collection of personal experiences and opinions aimed at fostering understanding and equality.

Gossip blogs (7)

Bricks and Stones bricksandstones.blogspot.com
Young Hollywood revealed.

Defamer www.defamer.com
Hollywood stars and hanger-ons bathe in the spotlight of this uber-popular Los Angeles gossip rag.

Gawker www.gawker.com
Gawker primarily focuses on Manhattan media news, but also covers celebrity sightings, scandals, and plenty of hearsay.

Go Fug Yourself gofugyourself.typepad.com
Based on the notion that you feel better about yourself when celebrities are caught wearing sweatpants.

Pink Is The New Blog www.pinkisthenewblog.com
Trent, the self-proclaimed "Pinkness of Power", relates the hottest celebrity gossip with his uniquely loving touch.

Reality Blurred www.realityblurred.com/realitytv
Daily digest of reality TV news.

The Superficial www.thesuperficial.com
Feeling unattractive? If not, big media hasn't worked its poison on you.

Insider blogs (7)

A Whole Lotta Nothing a.wholelottanothing.org
Mathowie (aka Matt Haughey) founded Metafilter and adds to his rep with a whole lot of nothing.

Anil Dash www.dashes.com/anil
Blogging A-lister and VP of Six Apart writes about technology, culture, politics, and art.

Biz Stone bizstone.com
Blog pioneer (helped start Xanga, worked at Google/Blogger) and author of two blog books.

Jason Calacanis www.calacanis.com
The personal blog of Weblogs, Inc. CEO Jason Calacanis provides insight into the continuing evolution of the blogosphere.

Megnut www.megnut.com
Personal blog of Meg Hourihan, co-founder of Pyra, the company that created Blogger. Topics range from food and travel to technology and women's rights.

Mena's Corner www.sixapart.com/about/corner
Mena Trott, president and co-founder of Six Apart (Movable Type, TypePad, Live Journal), keeps up with the blogosphere and shows off the inner workings of her start-up company.

Rebecca's Pocket www.rebeccablood.net
Writer, speaker, and blogging pioneer Rebecca Blood's personal blog. Author of *The Weblog Handbook* and the oft-linked "Weblogs: A History and Perspective" article.

Knitting blogs (3)

Knitting in Color knittingincolor.blogspot.com
From handspun yarns dyed with Kool-Aid to advice on the filet crochet.

Men Who Knit www.menwhoknit.com
Men from everywhere come together to exchange patterns and offer advice (includes instructions on knitting a stuffed pig).

Xtreme-Knitting Blog! www.xtreme-knitting.com/blog
This blog like totally rocks extreme to the max!

Law blogs (5)

Anonymous Lawyer anonymouslawyer.blogspot.com
Tales from the inside, written by a fictional hiring partner at a large law firm in a major city.

Groklaw www.groklaw.net
Journalist with a paralegal background provides detailed analysis on news from the industry.

Law Professors Blog www.lawprofessorblogs.com
Paul L. Caron and company maintain this scholarly blawg intended for those of us with some grounding in legal theory.

Lawrence Lessig www.lessig.org/blog
A Professor of Law at Stanford University, Lessig blogs about the intersection of law and technology.

Netlawblog www.netlawblog.com
Practical applications of the Internet, for lawyers.

Link blogs (10)

2xy www.2xy.org
Snarky link blog covering a wide variety of topics.

Boing Boing www.boingboing.net
"A Directory of Wonderful Things."

Danelope www.foreword.com/danelope.php
Links to the geekiest technology items on the Web.

Fark.com www.fark.com
A widely read community of the bizarre arranged by topic (including the likes of obvious, asinine, and boobies).

Guardian Unlimited Blogs blogs.guardian.co.uk
UK newspaper's main blog site draws headlines from its peripheral blogs in technology, politics, games, and more.

Kottke.org www.kottke.org
Highly influential and popular blogger links and opines about the world at large.

Metafilter www.metafilter.com
A hugely popular community weblog used for sharing links and discussing interesting sites.

Psionic www.psionic.nu
Tim links to the best pop culture, business, and political stories of the day.

Queerty www.queerty.com
Free of agenda. Except that gay one.

Sites and Soundbytes www.greenlakelibrary.org/blog
The director of a public library in Wisconsin maintains this link blog to interesting places on the web.

Literary blogs (7)

Bookslut www.bookslut.com/blog
One of the most popular literary blogs, Jessa Crispin oversees a constant stream of reviews, interviews, and industry news.

Confessions of an Idiosyncratic Mind www.sarahweinman.com/
You don't know crime fiction until you've read this site.

Elegant Variation marksarvas.blogs.com/elegvar
Screenwriter, short-story writer, and novelist Mark Sarvas delivers a Los Angeles perspective on the literary scene.

Galleycat www.mediabistro.com/galleycat
Excellent blog about books and publishing delivered with humor and wit.

Literary Saloon www.complete-review.com/saloon
Step us to the bar for a shot of literary news with a book review chaser.

Maud Newton maudnewton.com/blog
New Yorker Maud has been blogging about books and publishing since 2002.

Old Hag www.theoldhag.com
Topics range from literary matters to the arts and general culture. Features a 150-word book review column, Speedreader.

Metro blogs (7)

Gapers Block www.gapersblock.com
From 'da Bears to the blues, all things Chicago.

Gothamist www.gothamist.com
An award-winning blog about New York City and everything that happens in it. News, events, restaurants, bars, happenings, and goings-on.

Londonist www.londonist.com
Everything in, of, and about the Big Smoke.

Metroblogging www.metroblogging.com
Plugged in bloggers from forty cities worldwide are compiled and featured together.

New Yorkology www.newyorkology.com
Freelance writer Amy's exploration of New York City with posts about food, shops, sights, and travel.

SFGate Culture Blog sfgate.com/blogs/culture
If you're going to San Francisco…

Toronto Blog www.blogto.com
With an extensive Toronto blogroll and comprehensive event listings, this site shows that Toronto is more than just hockey and the CN Tower.

Miscellaneous interest blogs (15)

Apartment Therapy www.apartmenttherapy.com
Simple, functional designs and advice for making the most of your space.

Craftster www.craftster.org/blog
Crafter.org is a forum for people who love to make things with their own two hands, including clothing, toys, jewelry, and papercrafts.

Cute Overload mfrost.typepad.com/cute_overload
Worth it for the Rules of Cuteness alone.

Daily Rx time.blogs.com/daily_rx
Time magazine's daily notes on health and medicine.

Dilbert Blog dilbertblog.typepad.com
Scott Adams has a lot more to say than his strip will allow.

Gridskipper www.gridskipper.com
An off-the-track guide to the world's major urban dwellings.

Imomus imomus.livejournal.com
Eclectic musician travels about the globe, visiting installations and enjoying music from Japan to Germany.

Japundit www.japundit.com
A touch of Japan written in the English language.

Lost Remote www.lostremote.com
Keeping up with the latest trends and technology in TV and new media.

Make: Blog www.makezine.com/blog
DIY instructions for vibrating lock picks, copper-pipe potato guns, hoverboards, MP3 players, and so on.

Needled www.needled.com
Marisa DiMattia is a New York attorney and the author of *Tattoo Law*, a look at the art, culture, and politics of tattoos.

Post Secret postsecret.blogspot.com
An ongoing community art project – people mail in their secrets on a postcard, and they're posted anonymously.

Pop Candy blogs.usatoday.com/popcandy
Best used catching your mother up on pop culture.

Penny Arcade www.penny-arcade.com
The creators of the popular Penny Arcade Web comic highlight interesting tidbits from the Web.

Weblogg-ed www.weblogg-ed.com
Will Richardson's clear and direct advice on employing blogs as learning tools in schools.

Oddities (3)

Paranormal Magazine www.paranormalmagazine.com
Collects occurrences of the unexplained and connects them to long-running conspiracies, dark magic, and extraterrestrials.

Strange New Products www.strangenewproducts.com
Cat-claw caps, chocolate-filled diapers, diamond-filtered vodka, music composed from stock market data, and many similar items are reviewed for your enjoyment.

The Wild Hunt www.wildhunt.org/blog.html
Connecting paganism to everyday life.

Personal (21)

Adam Curry www.curry.com
Podcasts abound in former MTV VJ and Podcasting pioneer Adam Curry's blog.

Bazima www.bazima.com
Longtime blogger Blaise K. shares entertaining anecdotes about living in NYC.

Boygirlparty www.livejournal.com/users/boygirlparty
Personal weblog of Susie – illustrator, animal lover, roller-skater, and musician extraordinaire.

Bluish Orange www.bluishorange.com
Award-winning blog by Alison, a freelance web designer, writer, and jewelry maker based out of Houston.

Dooce www.dooce.com
Famously fired for maintaining a blog, Heather B. Armstrong consistently wins accolades for her humor and writing.

Eidolon eidolon-ink.blogspot.com
Wonderfully composed and entertaining blog about life, boys, and post-college trauma.

Evhead www.evhead.com
Nebraska boy makes it big. Evan Williams, co-founder and CEO of Pyra Labs (the maker of Blogger), on blogging advances and his new company, Odeo, Inc.

Ftrain.com www.ftrain.com
Paul Ford's real-life stories, written in collaboration with Scott Rahin and Rebecca Dravos (both completely fictional characters, by the way).

Greek Tragedy stephanieklein.blogs.com
Written by Manhattanite Stephanie Klein – the "Carrie Bradshaw" of bloggers.

Joe.My.God joemygod.blogspot.com
Stories about self-loathing, self-loving, family, drugs, sex, disease, and disco.

Little Yellow Different www.littleyellowdifferent.com
Famous for his humorous posts, Ernie Hsiung has won numerous awards for design, writing, and overall greatness.

Loobylu www.loobylu.com
Australian illustrator and toy maker Claire Robertson has won many awards for her whimsical drawings and beautifully constructed blog.

Maganda today.maganda.org
Christine mulls over fleeting interests and her love of crafts.

Minjung Kim www.minjungkim.com
Flat-chested, kimchi-squatting freak magnet contemplates life and love.

Plasticbag www.plasticbag.org
Maintained by influential English blogger Tom Coates, winner of numerous awards for his design, unique posts, and overall contribution to the genre.

Sinosplice www.sinosplice.com
Observations on life and language from a student of applied linguistics living in China.

Technicolor www.technicolor.org
University student Alexandra blogs from both sides of the Pacific.

Transcended www.transcended.net
The personal stories and political convictions of a conservative youth.

Whatever www.scalzi.com/whatever
Writer John Scalzi maintains this entertaining blog focused mainly on his job as an author.

Wockerjabby www.wockerjabby.com
Well-written and insightful journal blog of Rabi, dealing with family, friends, and her autoimmunity.

Xiaxue xiaxue.blogspot.com
Award-winning blog by Singaporean graphic arts student who tends to doll herself up (to the delight of fanboys everywhere).

Pets (4)

Dog Blog www.i-love-dogs.com/dog_blog
Worldwide dog happenings with links to products and reviews.

Entirely Pets pet.taragana.net
This blog specializes in all types of animal news from around the globe.

Music and Cats musicandcats.com
The living embodiment of Schweitzer's assertion.

What the Pets!? whatthepets.blogspot.com
Immerse yourself in this humorous pet blog – the Infinite Cat Project to "How to Use a Hamster Ball".

Photoblogs (13)

Ancient Imagery of the Future photoblog.hinius.net
Featuring monochromatic photographs of London street scenes.

Catherine Jamieson www.catherinejamieson.com
Daily updates include art photography, portraiture, slice-of-life pics, and mixed media images.

Chromasia www.chromasia.com/iblog
One of the most beautifully designed photoblogs around, with (of course), beautiful photographs.

Daily Dose of Imagery wvs.topleftpixel.com
Sam Javanrouh documents his day-to-day visual experience in Toronto.

Express Train www.travisruse.com
A great site if you like the idea of the NYC subway, but don't mind missing out on the smell of stale urine.

Lomo Playground playground.lomo.jp/ph
Takashi documents the Lomographies he takes with his Lomo LC-A.

Photoblogs.org www.photoblogs.org
An overwhelmingly extensive collection of photoblogs.

Photojunkie www.photojunkie.ca
Bloggie award winner for Best Canadian Blog in 2003 and 2005.

Quarlo www.quarlo.com
An old-school devotee, Todd Gross shoots his pictures on standard film, and then scans in the developed photos.

Rion.nu www.rion.nu
Street photographer Rion Nakaya takes on New York City.

Shutterbug www.sh1ft.org/shutterbug
2004 Bloggie award winner Tracey posts pictures of her everyday life in Sydney, Australia.

Shutterbug.nu shutterbug.nu
Nilesh Chaudhari's engaging pictures of Southeast Asia and India helped him to the 2005 Photobloggies award.

Ten Years of My Life www.tenyearsofmylife.com
Matthew Haughey is posting one photo for every day he survives over the next ten years.

Political blogs (32)

Andrew Sullivan www.andrewsullivan.com
Andrew Sullivan, journalist and blog celebrity, writes about politics, homosexuality, the mass media, and many other topics.

Blog For America www.blogforamerica.com
In search of a centralizing tenet for the Democratic Party.

Brad DeLong's Semi-Daily Journal
www.j-bradford-delong.net/movable_type
Professor of Economics at UC Berkeley examines the intersection of politics and economics.

Crooks and Liars www.crooksandliars.com
Political vlog providing links, news, and commentary on television segments and policy debates.

Daily Kos www.dailykos.com
One of the largest and most influential liberal group blogs features posts from readers alongside commentary and analysis from Markos Moulitsas.

Eschaton atrios.blogspot.com
Recovering economist provides left-leaning analysis on media and politics.

Huffington Post www.huffingtonpost.com
Part news aggregator and part group blog, the Huffington Post is the
brainchild of nationally syndicated columnist Arianna Huffington and
features entries from the likes of David Geffen, Tina Brown, John Cusack,
Vernon Jordan, Norman Mailer, and more.

Hugh Hewitt www.hughhewitt.com
Conservative radio host blogs about politics, media, and culture.

Hullabaloo digbysblog.blogspot.com
Popular left-wing blog featuring blunt analysis of the Republican agenda
and the Democratic disconnection with Middle America.

Instapundit www.instapundit.com
Political weblog produced by Glenn Reynolds, a Law professor at the
University of Tennessee. One of the most widely read blogs in the world.

Kaus Files www.kausfiles.com
A "mostly political" blog written by Mickey Kaus, author and journalist,
featured on Slate.com. One of the first political blogs to hit the blogosphere.

Librarian.net www.librarian.net
Jessamyn West, rural librarian, is a self-described anti-capitalist blogger
who started her blog in response to the individual library records searches
made possible by the US Patriot Act.

Little Green Footballs www.littlegreenfootballs.com/blog
Very popular and widely read political blog run by Web designer Charles
Johnson. Provides extensive commentary on US domestic and interna-
tional politics.

Michelle Malkin www.michellemalkin.com
Right-wing blogger, book author, and journalist is always ready to stir up
trouble.

the blogroll

Orcinus dneiwert.blogspot.com
Long scholarly posts on public policy, politics, culture, and journalism.

Political Animal www.washingtonmonthly.com
Kevin Drum used to run a popular liberal-leaning blog, Calpundit. After finding sponsorship, he moved and renamed his blog accordingly.

Power Line www.powerlineblog.com
Named *Time* magazine's Blog of the Year 2004, Power Line is a conservative blog run by three lawyers covering political and social issues.

Redstate www.redstate.org
A community weblog dedicated to the ideals of neocon strategist Karl Rove.

Talking Points Memo www.talkingpointsmemo.com
Prominent political blogger Joshua Micah Marshall's blog focuses on politics, culture, and foreign affairs.

Talk Left www.talkleft.com
Thoroughly examines issues, candidates, and legislative initiatives as they pertain to constitutional rights, particularly those of persons accused of criminal acts.

The American Prospect www.prospect.org/weblog
Exposing the stealth agendas, fear-mongering tactics, and secret propaganda apparatus of the neocons.

The Corner www.nationalreview.com/thecorner/corner.asp
The National Review Online's conservative, multi-authored blog.

The Peking Duck www.pekingduck.org
Personal blog from an American expat living in Asia explores consistencies between Bush and Hu Jintao.

The Reality-Based Community www.samefacts.com
UCLA public policy professor blogs about terrorism and teaching.

The Truth Laid Bear www.truthlaidbear.com
Blog portal tracking political news with excellent navigation functions and community-building features.

This Modern World www.thismodernworld.com
Political commentator Dan Perkins' weekly satirical comic strip attacks the circular logic of the conservative agenda.

Tony Blair's Campaign Diary www.labour.org.uk/tonyblair
Can the Labour Party really secure Britain's future?

TPM Café www.tpmcafe.com
Companion site to Joshua Marshall's Talking Points Memo. Forum for commentary, discussion, collaborative journalism, and political activism.

Volokh Conspiracy www.volokh.com
UCLA law professor and his students discuss constitutional, criminal, and copyright law.

Wampum wampum.wabanaki.net
A blog focusing on progressive politics and Native American Indian issues.

Whiskey Bar www.billmon.org
Tongue-in-cheek political analysis.

Wonkette www.wonkette.com
The Wonkette team presents political analysis and backroom DC gossip with almost pornographic intensity.

Pundit blogs (11)

Blogcritics www.blogcritics.org
A collection of bloggers critique music, books, film, popular culture, politics, and technology.

the blogroll

Buzz Machine www.buzzmachine.com
Former TV critic Jeff Jarvis writes with a focus on journalism, politics, and entertainment.

Dialog Now www.dialognow.org
Conceived as a forum for Indian and Pakistani dialogue, the site now hosts conversations about any number of topics specific to South Asia.

Freakonomics: Blog www.freakonomics.com/blog
Part book promotion, part critique of daily economic events.

Informed Comment www.juancole.com
Juan Cole, University of Michigan professor, blogs about the Middle East, history, and religion.

James Wolcott www.jameswolcott.com
Contributing editor to *Vanity Fair* writes on topics ranging from economics and politics to media and pop culture.

Rashmi Sinha www.rashmisinha.com
Thoughts on technology, design, and cognition. Includes topics like "The Visualization of Valentine's Day" and "Neuroscience comes to the Superbowl."

Romenesko www.poynter.org/column.asp?id=45
Daily fix of media industry news, commentary, and memos.

The Uber Geeks www.theubergeeks.net
A blog by three geeks in love with music and the Macintosh.

Tuned In time.blogs.com/tuned_in
All thing television by *Time* magazine's TV critic.

VH1's Best Week Ever Blog bestweekever.blogs.com
VH1's popular show shortens its timeframe, recaps late-breaking celebrity news you may have missed while watching *Oprah*.

Sex blogs (3)

Eros Blog: The Sex Blog www.erosblog.com
Everything and anything about sex – includes animated ASCII pole-dancing.

NY Hotties www.nyhotties.com
The confessionals of a NYC escort.

SexBlo.gs www.sexblo.gs
Mixing artistic expression and hardcore action, this site challenges the traditional understanding of sexual congress.

Sports blogs (9)

Blog FC blogfc.com/theblog
News and views about soccer in England and beyond.

Sports Blog Nation www.sbnation.com
A baseball blog with a smattering of other sports when America's game isn't in season.

Sports Blogs www.sportsblogs.org
The People's Sports Network aggregates over a thousand sports blogs from around the country.

Sports Frog www.sportsfrog.com
Commentary that can only be the result of endless hours spent watching Sportscenter.

Sports Law Blog sports-law.blogspot.com
Increasingly important in today's multi-billion-dollar professional sports industry.

The Soxaholix www.soxaholix.com
Daily comic strip set in a generic office, inhabited by a collection of die-hard Red Sox supporters.

The Sports Economist www.thesportseconomist.com
Clemson University economics professor discusses the financial impact of modern sports.

True Hoop www.truehoop.com
NBA news from longtime sports journalist Henry Abbott.

Yanksfan vs Soxfan yanksfansoxfan.typepad.com/ysfs
Longtime rivalry finds its most impotent form of expression.

Tech blogs (18)

Anne's Weblog about Markup and Style annevankesteren.nl
Anne van Kesteren explores all the Web standards, including XML, XHTML, and CSS.

Ars Technica www.arstechnica.com
Focusing on the PC enthusiast, Ken Fischer and crew consolidate hardware and software news and reviews.

Digital Photography Blog www.livingroom.org.au/photolog
If you are buying a camera, this is your blog. Includes digital camera reviews and ratings, tips, and side-by-side comparisons via pricescan.com.

Engadget www.engadget.com
A giant in the world of gadget/electronics blogs. They cover cell phones, videogames, tech toys, and produce an excellent Podcast.

Gizmodo www.gizmodo.com
Always on the cutting edge.

Google Blog googleblog.blogspot.com
Official Google weblog, with news of new products, events, and glimpses of life inside the Googleplex.

iLounge www.ilounge.com
All things iPod, iTunes, iEtc.

Kuro5hin www.kuro5hin.org
Technology and tech culture – from the trenches.

Life Hacker www.lifehacker.com
Life Hacker recommends computer downloads, websites, and shortcuts designed to cut out repetitive tasks.

Make You Go Hmm www.makeyougohmm.com
News and links with insightful commentary on tech culture.

PVR Blog www.pvrblog.com
Everything you need to know about personal video recorders (with a particular slant toward TiVo), including industry news and how-to guides.

Slashdot www.slashdot.org
A highly trafficked blog covering tech advances, space travel, aliens – pretty much every topic you'd want to avoid on a first date.

Tech Confidential blogs.thedeal.com
This weblog mixes technology and corporate finance news.

TechCrunch www.techcrunch.com
TechCrunch profiles and reviews new Web 2.0 (post-dot.com collapse) products and companies.

Techdirt www.techdirt.com
News, commentary, and discussions on the most important (and entertaining) high-tech news.

The Cult of Mac Blog blog.wired.com/cultofmac
Furthering Steve Jobs' agenda from inside *Wired*.

The Gadgeteer www.the-gadgeteer.com
Judie and Julie review sleek new handhelds and accessories.

Unofficial Apple Weblog (TUAW) www.tuaw.com
A whole host of contributors share their knowledge of Mac products and events, while offering plenty of tips and advice.

Personal tech blogs (6)

C:/Pirillo.exe chris.pirillo.com
Chris Pirillo, technology guru and famous blogger, presents problems and fixes for apps and hardware with an occasional dip into US football fanaticism.

Doc Searls doc.weblogs.com
The well-respected Doc Searls taps various muses in his blog of many topics.

Joi Ito joi.ito.com
Joi Ito – activist, entrepreneur, venture capitalist, and pioneering blogger.

Micro Persuasion www.micropersuasion.com
One of the most popular bloggers in the world, Steve Rubel explores how new technologies are transforming marketing, media, and public relations.

Scobleizer scobleizer.wordpress.com
Microsoft employee and all-around geek Robert Scoble maintains this popular personal blog with a heavy focus on blogging, tech updates, and, of course, Microsoft.

Scripting News www.scripting.com
One of the first bloggers, Dave Winer is the software pioneer responsible for many innovations used by bloggers (Radio Userland, RSS, Podcasting). Dave's blog focuses on general computer industry links, Podcasting, and tech advances.

Video blogs (7)

Karmagrrrl www.smashface.com/vlog
Rocketboom's LA correspondent Zadi Diaz's personal vlog.

Michael Verdi www.michaelverdi.com
Vlogging to make the world a better place.

Minnesota Stories www.mnstories.com
An evolving experiment in decentralized citizen media.

Mom's Brag Vlog nealey.blogspot.com
Vlog by a mother of two sharing precious moments with her children's grandparents.

Rocketboom www.rocketboom.com
Three-minute daily vlogs with a heavy emphasis on international arts, technology, and weblog drama.

Scratch Video scratchvideo.tv
New York documentary film editor by day, experimental vlogger by night.

Taylor Street Studio www.taylorstreetstudio.com
Pioneering Portland vlogger explores the storytelling and distribution possibilities of online syndicated cinema.

Video games blogs (4)

Joystiq www.joystiq.com
Gamers are taken seriously in this incredibly comprehensive blog.

Kotaku www.kotaku.com
Snuggled warmly under the wing of Gawker, this in-depth videogaming blog posts lots of images and is always in on the latest releases.

The Ludologist www.jesperjuul.net/ludologist
A critical take on the personal and social ramifications of increasing realistic videogames.

ButtonMashing.com buttonmashing.com
Basing its name on a highly successful NES technique, this blog documents the daily obssesions of a hard-core gamer.

Work/job blogs (6)

I Work With Fools www.iworkwithfools.com
Anonymous posters rant about their idiotic bosses and co-workers.

JobStuff, A Blog for Your Career jobstuff.blogdrive.com
Stephen Harris reassures and advises "transition-zone" job hunters.

LifeWork Design lifeworkdesign.blogspot.com
A career development counselor gives job-hunting advice and chats with commenters.

Monster Blog monster.typepad.com/monsterblog
Further suggestions by members of Monster.com's career advice team.

Occupational Adventure Blog curtrosengren.typepad.com
Try turning your everyday passions into a salaried adventure.

Work-Related Blogs and News workblogging.blogspot.com
Links to blogs penned by police officers, coroners, firefighters, teachers, and truck drivers, among many other occupations.

Index

Index

9/11 10, 124, 137

A

about page 84–85
ad-free blogs 36
AdBrite 103
Adopt a Blog 132
advertising 30, 102, 148
aggregators 23, 41, 54
Alavi, Nasrin 125
Amazon Associates 103
American Idol Blog 121
AmphetaDesk 25
Anderson, Chris 164
Anti-Bloggies 18
Apache 45
archives 73–74
Arden, Jann 165
Armstrong, Heather B. 104
art blogs 161

Audacity 57
audience-building 87
AudBlog 52
AudioBlog 52
audioblogs 6, 52
Audio Blogger 52

B

Backfence 135
Baghdad Blogger 12
bandwidth 46
Barger, Jorn 4
Barry, Dave 120, 165
Belle de Jour 107, 116
Berkeley Blogs 144
Berners-Lee, Tim 75
Blair, Jayson 13
Blair, Tony 183
blawgs 152
Blogads 103

index

Blogger 36–37
Bloggies, The 17
BlogJet 50
Bloglines 24
blogorrhea 81
Blogpulse 21
blogrolls 76, 95, 161
blogs
  awards 17–18
  creating 6, 29–79
  elements of 61–65
  etymology of 4
  naming conventions 30
  number of 6
  review sites 19
  search engines 20–21
  templates 33, 69–71
  writing 80–87
BlogSkins 69
Blog For America 15, 128
Blog Meetup 113
Blog of the Day 19
Blog Patrol 91
blog portals 9, 20
blog rings 21
Blood, Rebecca 170
book publishers 107
borders 77
Braff, Zach 166
Brighton's Hope 141
Brown, Jerry 135
building communities 112–113
Bush, George W.
  campaign blog 128
  environmental concerns 135
  fantasy blog 117
  Google bomb 94
  march to war 14
  National Guard service 12
  Saudi princes 127
Business Blogging Index 147
business blogs 146, 163
Buzznet 43
buzz sites 149
Byrne, David 165

C

CafePress 101
Cancer Blog, The 117
car blogs 164
celebrity blogs 120, 165
CEOs 156
Cho, Margaret 121
Coates, Tom 18
college blogs 143
comments 65, 70, 96
comment spam 70
Commission Junction 103
Coudal 152
CQ Counter 91
CreateBlog 70
Cuban, Mark 156
Curbed 154
Curry, Adam 55
Customer Evangelists 152
customer service 150
Cutler, Jessica 105

D

Dallas Mavericks 156
Dateline Earth 135
date and time stamp 64
Daypop 21
Dean, Howard 15, 128
Defamer 106
Democracy for America 15
Derakhshan, Hossein 126
desktop publishing tools 50
Diaryland 42
Dibbell, Julian 118
DomainDirect 46
domain names 29, 39, 44, 153
domain registrars 45
donations 100
Dooce 104
Doppler 55
Doteasy 46
Dreamhost 46
Drudge, Matt 127
Drudge Report, The 127
Dualstar 120

E

East/West 112
EasyMoblog 43
Eaton, Brigitte 9
Eatonweb Portal 21
eBay 118
Edelman, Richard 156

elementary school 140
email 35, 39, 41, 42, 66
Engadget 120, 186
Expression Engine 49

F

Fantastico 46
fantasy blogs 117
Fast Company 16, 151
FeedBurner 58
Feedster 20
Fetus Spears 117
Firefox 24
Fitzpatrick, Brad 39
fonts 66–68
food blogs 167
footers 63
Frank the Goat 40
Frat Pack, The 120
freedom of expression
    China 131
    Iran 130
Free Republic 127
Free Vlog 60
Fresh Inc 154
Friendster 42
FTP 9, 34, 46

G

gadget blogs 120
Gaiman, Neil 166

index

Gannon, Jeff 134
Gawker Media 103, 106, 107, 164, 189
Gibson, Todd 162
Gibson, William 166
Gizmodo 106, 120, 186
Global Voices Online 22, 136
GM's Fastlane 147
Google
  AdSense 102
  Blogger purchase 36
  blog registry 93
  Blog Search 20–22
  Googleplex 155
  Google bombing 94
  Google Reader (RSS) 24
gossip blogs 83, 168
grassroots journalism 135
Grates, Gary 147
Greek Tragedy 107
Green, Tyler 162
Grey, Noah 49
Greymatter 49
Groklaw 153
Guardian, The 12, 15, 18, 171

H

Hall, Justin 10
Haloscan 71
Hanscom, Michael 105
headers 61
hits 91
hobby blogs 118

Hoder 126
homepages 8
Hourihan, Meg 169
HTML 9, 74–76
Huba, Jackie 152
Huffington, Arianna 181

I

Ice Rocket 21
images 76–79
Instapundit 129
Internet Explorer 24
iPods 18, 53, 55
iPodder 55
IP addresses 92
iTunes 54

J

Jello Biafra 135
Jordan, Eason 134
journal blogs 10, 111–115
jPodder 55
Just Jared 120

K

K-blogs 158
Kaus, Mickey 13
Klein, Stephanie 107, 177
knitting blogs 170

Korean Blog List, The 125
Kottke, Jason 100
Kuro5hin 120

L

law blogs 152, 170
Lewinsky, Monica 127
Liberated Syndication 58
Lincoln Sign Company 155
links 86
link blogs 171
link etiquette 96
literary blogs 172
LiveJournal 39
Lott, Trent 13, 128
Lutz, Bob 147

M

MacKinnon, Rebecca 136
Manilow, Barry 165
marketing with blogs 148
Marshall, Joshua Micah 13
Mathes, Adam 94
McConnell, Ben 152
McCullagh, Declan 153
McKellen, Ian 165
Mediabistro 107
merchandising 101
Merholz, Peter 5
micropatrons 100
Microsoft 131

milblogs 125–127
Minnesota 189
MixCast Live 57
moblogging 43
Money Pit, The 118
Movable Type 38, 47
Mraz, Jason 165
MyBlueDots 37
Myspace 42

N

National Review 129
Nee Naw 116
New York Times 13, 134
Nimiq 55
Nokia 149
Not (that) Ugly 70
NWA Voices 142
NYC Bloggers 113

O

odd blogs 175
Odeo 55, 58
Oliver, Jamie 166

P

PageRank 94
page views 91
page visits 91

index

Pavlina, Steve 164
Pax, Salam 12, 125
PayPal 101
permalinks 7, 65
Perreault, John 161
photoblogs 114, 178
Picasa 37
Pink Is The New Blog 169
Pitas 9
pixels 68
Play Money 118
plug-ins 24, 48, 49
pMachine 49
Podcast.net 56
Podcasting News 56
Podcasts 53–58, 138, 144, 411
Podcast Alley 56
Podomatic 58
points 68
political blogs 124–132, 180
posts 63
post titles 64, 85–86
Potts, Mark 135
Powell, Julia 107
PressThink 136
Primal Records 146
privacy 115
product enhancement 151
professional blogs 116
project blogs 158
pull quotes 64
pundits 10
  right vs. left 127–128
PVRblog 16

Q

Queen of Sky 104
QuickPost 38

R

Radio Userland 41
Raging Cow 150
Raines, Howell 13
Rather, Dan 13, 127
RConversation 136
realty blogs 153
Research Blogs 144
Robertson, Claire 177
Robinson, James 127
Rocketboom 60
Rogers, Betsy 141
Romenesko 13
RSS 23–25, 35, 58
  creating a feed 97

S

Safari 24
Salon 129
Scalzi, John 178
Schwartz, Jonathan 156
Scoble, Robert 16, 155
ScrapBook 39
server-side blogging 44–50

servers 45
sex blogs 114, 185
ShoutFish 116
sidebars 62
sideblogs 71
Sitemeter 90
site counters 91
Six Apart 38
skinning 69
Slashdot 119
Smith, Keri 162
Socialtext 147
Soft Skull Press 125
source code 33
Spears, Britney 117
Spectator, The 129
spidering 93
Spiers, Elizabeth 107
sports blogs 122, 185
Star Trek 11
Stone, Biz 169
Studio Four-News 140
Sullivan, Andrew 13, 136
Sun Microsystems 156
SXSW 17, 113
syndication 23–25, 35, 58, 97

templates 38, 69–71
Template Hunter 70
Text America 43
Text messaging 39
Thurman, Strom 13
TrackBack 38
Trademark Blog, The 153
Trott, Ben 47
Trott, Mena 47, 170
TypeLists 38
TypePad 38

T

taglines 30
Talon News 134
Technorati 5
tech blogs 119, 186

U

Uber Geeks, The 184
Ultima Online 118
university blogs 143

V

vegans 167
Videoblogs 59–60, 189
Videoblog Directory, The 59
video game blogs 189

W

w.bloggar 50
Waldman, Simon 18
warblogs 12, 124–126
Washingtonienne, The 105, 107

index

Washington Post, The 135
Webbies, The 18
Weblogg-ed 138
weblogistan 130
Weblogs, Inc. 103, 106
Weblogs.com 56
Weblog Review, The 19
Weblog Wannabe 115
Web design 76
We Are Iran 125
Wheaton, Wil 11, 120
Williams, Evan 176
Winer, Dave 55
Wisconsin 172
Wonkette 106

WordPress 48
word verification 37

X

Xanga 40
 XTools 41

Y

Yahoo!
 blog registry 93
 Yahoo! 360° 42